Creative Sparks

Mishaps, hurdles and ideas
to inspire you and yours.

Here's to inspiring imaginations!
Sarah ★

mum and multi award-winning entrepreneur
Sarah Cressall

First published in Great Britain May 2018 by The Creation Station Ltd.

For information contact;
Address: Inspiration House, Creativity Drive, Woodbury Business Park, Woodbury, Devon EX5 1AY

www.thecreationstation.co.uk | 01395 239700
www.sarahcressall.co.uk
The Creation Station Ltd
@CreationStation
CreationStationInspiration

Book and cover design by Ramseys Design Lab

ISBN: 978-1-9999017-0-7

A dedication to:

Mum

Sam

Ollie

Josh

Duncan

to the moon

...and beyond

Foreword

Within five minutes of meeting Sarah in London I knew we were going to be friends. We settled down for a chat and three hours later we came up for air. Sarah has that natural ability to put you at your ease, listening attentively, laughing uproariously and insatiably curious to share life's adventures and stories with others. We weaved our way through our common passions and mutual experiences of life (well, we are women of a certain age!) and we had a little glass of wine. It was uplifting, inspiring and great fun!!

What shines through this wonderful book is that creativity is more than just making a funny hat or moulding a piece of clay. It's more than being 'good' at drawing a horse or painting a sunset. It's that creative spark within you that unleashes your spirit to explore, tinker, play, ponder and create, free from finger pointing or judgement. It's when you get lost in your own creative adventure and time flies.

It's where change happens, creativity soars, innovation is unleashed and confidence grows.

It's where kids make a mess and make mistakes. It's where they harness their imagination and express their unique creative potential through exploration and discovery. It's where 'out of the box' thinking is encouraged, nurtured and celebrated and where children become actively involved in the world around them.

Putting creativity back into childhood.

Creativity and creative intelligence is often misunderstood, undervalued and sidelined by our obsession with data driven learning and the busy-ness of modern life. In this hectic, frenetic 24/7 connected mobile world where family life seems busier than ever, it's even more important to make a conscious effort to allow your kids to play, have fun, explore and discover – to think for themselves and become confident in their own abilities to problem solve.

Bursting with simple, easy and fun activities this book will inspire you to explore new ideas, give you confidence to discover new things and empower you with new skills that will enrich the lives of your children and your whole family.

By embracing these creative experiences in childhood, you will benefit your children's mental, emotional and physical well-being throughout their entire lives.

In a world of growing uncertainty and where many parents work long hours, carving out meaningful family time takes thought, planning and discipline. The impact of watching devices in separate rooms and not eating together regularly, has had a massive impact on family connection in recent years, and it is why many children can feel disconnected, isolated and alone.

We are in need of simple and fun ways to equip children and young people with ways to feel resilient, resourceful, connected and able to unleash their creativity in new and exciting ways.

Never before have we needed more positive, creative ways to empower what I call a 'Can Do Kid' ready to embrace life.

Sarah's book opens a door to that creative mindset and helps you see the world in a more positive light.

'Creative Sparks' will empower a generation of children to become creative, innovative, independent, resourceful, resilient and confident in their own abilities to try new things, and be resourceful enough to tackle anything and able to bounce back after setbacks.

It will build the positive mindset, motivation and long-term self-confidence and self-worth that children need to succeed. There's a huge body of evidence that shows that encouraging children to be creative and imaginative early in life can actually help them to be more resourceful and resilient when they are faced with barriers or obstacles in adult life.

Why should creativity matter to kids? What's the big deal?

Toddlers and young children are masters of the moment – they love the way it feels when they smear paint on paper, or listen to the swooshing sound of a paintbrush as it gently glides across the page or how it looks when they sprinkle glitter with utter abandon over a large space with their fingers. Unlike older kids and most adults, toddlers and pre-schoolers aren't self-conscious about what they're doing or focused on creating a finished product. They're simply enjoying the process. They are in the magic of creating, so allowing children of all ages to enjoy the process of creation can reap huge rewards emotionally, socially, intellectually and spiritually, particularly if we as parents give them attention, encouragement and freedom to explore.

When children explore their creativity, they unlock their potential to dream without limits, believe in themselves and achieve amazing things. This book takes you all on a fascinating journey of exploration where you can all blossom, bloom and thrive.

Sarah harnesses the power to think, create, connect and inspire.

Sarah's philosophy and vision of putting creativity back into childhood, and throughout life, through 'Tiny Treasures' 'Baby Discover', 'Little Explorer', 'Family Fun' or Prosecco drinking 'Creative Crafters' sessions or 'Care and Creativity' intergenerational fun in care homes, creates safe spaces to let people discover the simple power of their own creativity. This is truly life enhancing, transforming and awe inspiring.

This is a book to inspire you with a new approach to thinking about creativity that will enhance your enjoyment of life.

As Sarah unfolds the layers of her own life's experiences and lessons, she offers you the opportunity to 'Pause to Ponder' your own, making this an interactive, thought-provoking book of 'aha' moments for you too.

Whether it's trying some of the activities included in the book at home, joining a class or experience near you, or even deciding to run your own Creation Station franchise you can unleash your creativity and inspire your children to explore and release theirs too.

This wonderfully warm, funny, moving book is bursting with inspirational life lessons alongside creative ideas for having fun with your kids. With its heart-warming stories, helpful tips and practical ideas this fabulous book will be on the bedside table of every parent or grandparent, well thumbed, highlighted and dog-eared for many years to come!

Sue Atkins

Sue Atkins
ITV 'This Morning' Parenting Expert and Author of 'Parenting Made Easy – How To Raise Happy Children' and The Sue Atkins Parenting Club: www.thesueatkins.com

Reviews

"Creativity is that magic spark that ignites the imagination & transforms the ordinary into the extraordinary"

"Sarah's book Creative Sparks is a lovely mix of inspirational life lessons and creative ideas. Her lesson's learnt, often the hard way, offer us space to consider our own life choices and show us how important it is to make creativity our constant companion. As a parent, Sarah has given me the space to consider the values I want to pass onto my children and heaps of ideas on bringing up a family with creative intelligence. If you believe that creativity and play are crucial to your child's development then this is the book for you."

Debra Searle MVO MBE
Solo Atlantic rower, British adventurer, television presenter, author and motivational speaker.
www.debrasearle.com

"Sarah's book will make you want to grab life and live it for all its worth! This wonderfully warm, sad, funny, emotional story of Sarah's life is complete proof that you can achieve anything and everything as long as you are prepared to work towards your goals and to be open-minded and open-hearted. It's a great tool to help you achieve your dreams and will inspire all generations of parents/grandparents to enable not just themselves, but their children/grandchildren to be the best they can be. I am not a parent but still loved the book and felt inspired with every new chapter of Sarah's life. Read it now and who knows where your dreams will take you!"

Anne Walker MBE
Founder of The International Dance Supplies, entrepreneur, mentor and coach.
www.annewalker.com

"If you are interested in understanding more about creativity, then this is the book for you. Lovely stories, helpful tips and practical activities."

Penny Mallory,
Former Rally Champion and TV Presenter.
www.pennymallory..co.uk

"I have long been an admirer of Sarah's creative abilities; we've enjoyed Creation Station activities as a family. Despite secondary school looming and mobile phones having taken over the world, there is nothing like the satisfaction of making something with their own bare hands to keep kids happy. The 'grown up' part of this book really got me thinking; "What WOULD I attempt to do if I knew I could not fail?" Fear of failure is something that holds all of us back, from kids to adults, and Sarah's natural enthusiasm makes all of us think that maybe we should just give it a go and see what happens? It's an inspiring book for the whole family, I loved it."

Andrea Mclean,
TV Presenter.

"This inspirational book shows the value of creativity in every aspect of life. From starting up in business, to developing an award-winning franchise, from raising a family to fulfilling your dreams. Sarah's journey is both immensely personal and hugely relatable."

Dr Amanda Gummer,
Fundamentally Children.

"I have known Sarah for a long time and she has always inspired me with her incredible creativity, amazing get up and go and love of a good laugh. This book highlights her knowledge and understanding of psychological processes such as the link between thoughts and feelings and how negative and restrictive thinking holds us back from our full potential. She recognises the importance of self-reflection and the power of self-compassion. Rather than learning through academic study, Sarah seems to have gained her insight through life experiences and giving herself time to think and reflect. This is a powerful way to learn. As well as being generous and kind to her friends, colleagues and personal causes. Sarah has always put her family first and prioritised the growth and development of her children, which is exactly the way things should be. Through play and creative exploration, she has developed with them attuned relationships which have allowed her to accurately guess what her kids need emotionally, as well as physically and educationally.

Sarah has used her knowledge to develop creative activities for children that enhance their emotional well-being, build relationships and stimulate creative and independent thinking. As a Clinical Psychologist and a Mum, I am looking forward to using some of the suggestions for creative activities in the book with my family, people I work with and colleagues."

Dr Kerry Davison,
Registered Clinical Psychologist.
BSc Hons, CPsychol, AFBPsS

"I am so thrilled that Sarah has finally been able to share her huge energies and creativity to an even greater audience through her engaging, informative and thought-provoking book. I always had her down as 'the Anita Roddick' of the creative world; and told her so many years ago when we were fellow members of the Entrepreneurs Circle She has gone on to inspire hundreds of thousands and has fully earnt that compliment. She's great fun and a legend in her time."

Dave Stickland,
Store Guru.

"I remember being in Sarah's very first Creation Station class back in September 2002 with my son Dan. It was really relaxed, very social and good fun. I loved having that special time with my son where we could get creative together, and I didn't have to plan the activities or do any of the clearing up. I can see why The Creation Station has taken off to be such a national success. The classes, parties and events are great for kids, loved by parents - and fun and educational too. It was great to be there right at the beginning and see it develop and grow."

Hillary Cole,
Attended the first Creation Station classes in 2002.

"I've not read a book that's combined telling a story with empowering the reader in this way before and I love it! Sarah first takes us on a fun adventure as we find out who she is and why she does what she does. Sarah weaves in moments for personal reflection with thought-provoking questions. Sarah's honest approach is helpful too as it can tap into the negative voices that might be running through our own heads. Not only does this book have the potential to inspire the next generation, I believe it will have a big role in inspiring parents and carers who don't feel that they are creative. So, I massively recommend this book to anyone who wants to spend fun time with children and to know that they're encouraging the development of valuable skills and thought processes at the same time. A must for all parents and a great gift idea too!"

Julia Bramble
BrambleBuzz

"Sarah's book Creative Sparks, really is an inspirational read. Not only for parents seeking creative ideas, but far more importantly for helping teach children about the importance of perseverance, mindset and creative thinking. In my work I see young people struggling to find their place in life and not knowing how to progress in their lives, sharing some of Sarah's work with them would make a huge difference."

Richard Daniel Curtis,
The Kid Calmer, leading child behaviour expert.

"Creative Sparks is such an honest, heart-warming and helpful read. As well as being packed full of ideas for nurturing and exploring creativity, Sarah's book also details her journey to becoming a highly successful entrepreneur whilst balancing an active and happy family life. She gives us an honest and open account of how she nurtured the kernel of an idea into a multi award-winning creative franchise. For anyone thinking of starting their own business, Sarah's book may provide just the encouragement and incentive you need. Her story is inspiring but also relatable, and brims with enthusiasm and positivity."

Gillian Nissim,
Founder - www.workingmums.co.uk

"An inspiring leader, entrepreneur and mum, Sarah Cressall's dedication to seeing all children's potential released comes through so well in this book. Sarah's positive attitude, hard work and determination not to let anything get in the way of her dreams is a great model for today's society. Her passion for all children (and their families) to experience and enjoy their huge creativity is wonderfully evident in this easy-to-read toolkit of ideas and activities. It's a must-have for both parents and professionals looking for stimulating ideas and oodles of fun to have with their creative little ones!"

Ruth Churchill-Dower,
Founder - Earlyarts.

Contents

Part 1: Sarah's story – lessons from a creative life **15**
- The day I turned ideas into chocolate 25
- Foundations for growth 34
- Hard decisions and choosing life 40
- Out in Africa with Operation Raleigh 61
- A different path 74
- Creativity meets business – completing the jigsaw 84
- Getting the best job in the world 92
- Am I doing it right? 100
- Setting goals and the birth of a creative business 108
- Discovering my first franchise owner 118
- Creative sparks 122
- Learning from setbacks 130
- Raising a family with creative intelligence 140
- Putting creativity back into childhood 151

Part 2: Why creativity matters **160**

Part 3: A parent's role in nurturing creativity **186**

Part 4: 52 Activities to inspire your child's creativity **220**

"Explore new ideas.
Discover new things.
Develop new skills.
Dream big.
Play hard.
Be true to you.
Life's a journey - choose your path."

– Sarah Cressall

Part 1

Sarah's story - lessons from a creative life

Your future is a blank canvas - what will you create with yours?

"This book is about an ordinary little girl from an ordinary family whose mum taught her to believe that anything was possible."

Strengthened by this belief, little Sarah Long was inspired to aim high. As a child she didn't know what was 'realistic'. Instead, her ambition matched the size of her dreams.

And her dreams were big... As a child of the '70s and '80s, Sarah was inspired by the great people she saw who had an impact by making a difference to others.

"If they can do it, then what's stopping me?"

As a result, Sarah was open to explore, discover, and learn from the wide range of opportunities that came her way – both here and abroad. With encouragement from her mum and family, Sarah grew up to have confidence in exploring and developing her ideas. She was able to overcome her shyness, learnt to feel the fear and used this to manage risk and step well out of her comfort zone. She learnt to believe in herself and collaborate with others to create bigger differences. Sarah discovered that dreaming big and applying a creative process of exploration, discovery and development created new opportunities, strengthened resolve, and could make the impossible possible.

Sarah began to understand how creativity had the power to change the world – and so she decided to inspire others to nurture and express their own creativity. And she was prepared to do everything in her power to make this vision become a reality.

Becoming a parent was the watershed moment for Sarah, which changed everything.

After meeting her life partner and husband Duncan and the birth of their three boys – Sam, Ollie, and Josh – Sarah was inspired to create an innovative business that changed her life as well as thousands of others.

Established in 2002, The Creation Station is a much loved brand and the UK's leading force for inspiring imaginations and nurturing creativity through the power of arts and crafts.

To date, through its fun multi award-winning educational programmes and activities, The Creation Station has helped inspire over 950,000 children and families through its family of over 150 friendly franchise owners working across the UK.

The Creation Station has a clear purpose – to inspire imaginations and nurture creativity. And as a side effect of this goal, The Creation Station is also empowering women and men to run their own creative businesses.

Thanks to big dreams, The Creation Station has nurtured, strengthened and unlocked the creativity and imagination of thousands of children, families, adults and the elderly. It's a force for good that's making the world a better place. After all, who knows what these amazing children and grown-ups may bring into the world as a result of their creative ideas.

Because when you encourage children and adults alike to develop their creative intelligence, anything is possible..."

What to expect in this book

The little Sarah you've just met is me.

Although I feel almost grown-up – I still have a lot of learning, loving and laughing to do!

Now I'm Sarah Cressall, the proud mum to Sam, Ollie, and Josh, and wife to my lovely hubby, Duncan. I feel privileged to be the founder of The Creation Station and to work alongside incredible Creation Station franchise owners, our Creative Hub head office team, fantastic suppliers and partners, and to meet and support so many wonderful children, families and adults across the UK.

I'm passionate about nurturing creativity, especially within children because I've seen for myself the enormous rewards a creative approach to life can bring. I believe if children (and us grown-ups) can tap into and develop our creative intelligence, we have a greater chance of feeling fulfilled. We're also more likely to achieve our potential – whilst doing our bit to create a positive impact where we can in our worlds.

I see life as an adventure. Our choices and the paths we take define our experiences and the life we live. They also impact those we know and meet.

On the journey, there are many challenges, successes, failures, happiness and heartbreaks, as well as high and low points. We all have our own tapestry of life with different threads woven through.

So by writing this book and sharing some of my life experiences, along with a range of ideas and activities with you, I hope to inspire you to rediscover your creative spark while revealing how easy it is to enrich your child's life with creativity.

I'm passionate about this because I've found a creative approach can and does unlock the wonder within. This is a favourite phrase Duncan uses when talking with our boys.

And as a parent or carer, you have the opportunity to embrace a vital role in nurturing this most important life skill in your children. I'm sure it won't come as a surprise to know that a child's creativity is hugely influenced by the experiences and opportunities they have as they grow up. And that's where us parents and carers come in... we all want to raise happy, healthy, fulfilled children – and a creative approach can help you achieve that.

And that's why it's my hope that this book will give you some ideas to help you show your child how to find their creative spark and then explore, discover, develop, and enjoy it. I truly believe this will help them navigate their own journey and choose rewarding and fulfilling paths on their life adventure.

So what's in this book?

1

In Part One I'll share snippets from my own creative journey with you. You'll be able to understand how a creative approach has influenced many of the paths I've taken. I'll explain how creative intelligence has been a guiding force and responsible for overcoming hurdles and for many of the things that I've dreamed, believed, and achieved. I'll also share some techniques and activities that you will be able to adapt and apply to your own circumstances.

2

In Part Two we'll explore why creativity matters. Once you discover the wide range of skills and attributes that a creative outlook can provide, I think you'll look at the importance and value of creative activities in a whole new way.

3

In Part Three we'll talk more about what you can do as a parent or carer to offer experiences and opportunities for your children to express their creativity.

4

Finally, in Part Four, I'll share 52 creative activities, that's one a week for the next twelve months, which you can explore with your child to help unlock the wonder within.

But before we get going I need to stress one important thing...

I'm not here to tell you how you should raise your child or what you should or shouldn't do. This isn't a 'this is the way to do it' kind of book. After all, YOU are the best judge of what your child or children need – call it parental instinct if you like.

Instead, I've created this book with the hope that it can serve as a framework for you – something concrete, which you can build upon. I know from working with thousands of parents over the years that many adults sometimes struggle with how to be creative or nurture their child's thinking skills.

So that's how I see my role and the value of this book for you...

It's here to help you discover more about the true power of a creative approach and ensure you're never short of ideas and activities to nurture and stimulate your child's amazing and enquiring mind.

I hope you're as excited as me about the possibilities for you and your children.

Have fun and enjoy yourself.

Here's to inspiring futures.

With love.

Sarah

Think left,
Think right and
think low and
think high.
Oh, the thinks
you can think
up if only
you try!

Dr Seuss
(1)

The day I turned a daydream into chocolate

The first time I experienced that creativity could spark change in my world was when I was nine.

It all started with a serious lack of chocolate!

My three brothers and two sisters didn't seem too worried about the absence of chocolate in our house. And as the youngest of six I didn't get a look in when it came to deciding how to spend the family budget! But day after day I was distracted by chocolate daydreams and yes, 'Charlie and the Chocolate Factory' by Roald Dahl was my favourite book! I even managed to star in a local drama production in Crosby Town Hall in Merseyside, as the chocolate mad Mike TV. I have fond memories of being part of that amateur production – apart from the night when I munched too much chocolate just before my lines. I did get a lot of laughs though, at least I was keeping in character!

However, that acting role was the closest I thought I would ever get to an abundance of chocolate. I couldn't pester my mum. Back in the late '70s she had far more important things to worry about than her youngest daughter's insatiable chocolate cravings.

You see my dad had recently passed away from cancer leaving mum to bring up six children by herself.

My mum had five of us in five years then I came along four years later. Now that I'm a mum to three boys I don't know how mum coped. She was AMAZING (and she still is) and is a huge inspiration to me and so many others.

Back then we lived in Bootle, Liverpool and didn't have a lot of money. But that didn't dampen our spirits in the least. We learnt to make do with what we did have. I know at times we were a bit different to other families. Not everyone had fancy fabric extensions on the bottom of their trousers. It meant my favourite green boiler suit lasted for years. A fashion style that with hindsight, I can see wasn't really ever going to catch on. Our packed lunches also had a touch of uniqueness and created much interest in the playground. You never knew what was going be in the home-made pasty treat... A favourite one was the baked beans pasty. Despite the obvious challenges (and grief), my childhood was great fun. In fact, I have countless happy memories of the mad adventures that me and my siblings got up to in the backyard and on the green across the road.

I remember one day when I was playing out in the street, my big sister Fran, who is the next one up from me and four years older, told me to turn around and stand with my right hand sticking out. Of course only too happy to play, I stood perfectly still, only to hear a chap with a very deep scouse voice say:

'You getting on or what girl?'

Yep, I was standing at the request only 56 bus stop, with my back to the oncoming traffic and of course the bus had stopped. Strangely, I couldn't see my sister anywhere, but I did hear a roar of hysterics coming from behind a nearby quivering bush.

Then there was that time she gave me a bowl of freezing water and told me to throw it all over myself. Of course when my turn was finished and I went to get some freezing water for Fran, oddly it was the end of the game. Strange! As kids, Fran and I had so much fun together. Fran is still as creative as ever and continues to be an amazing support to me. In fact, I don't know where The Creation Station would be without her! She's a true Mrs Fix It! For example, our TV wouldn't work a few years ago and the kids said, "Better call Aunty Fran, mum!" But I digress...

Let's get back to what was at the top of my nine-year-old mind!

While I understood that chocolate was out of the question, that didn't stop me dreaming about peeling off the wrapper and savouring the rich flavours of my favourite chocolate bar (and maybe even finding a golden ticket tucked away inside for an exciting adventure!)

And my desire to satisfy my sweet tooth got me thinking. There must be something I could do.

But what...?

For as long as I can remember, my mum had always told me that I could achieve anything I put my mind to. In fact, it's a message I still hear ringing in my ears to this day.

As an impressionable child who adored my mum, I believed every word she said (there's a lesson in there, which we'll come back to later).

I decided to contact people who I knew for certain had a lot of chocolate – chocolate factory workers. After all, the Cadbury's chocolate I saw in all the shops had to be made somewhere.

One rainy Saturday afternoon, my best friend Joanne and I got out our felt pens and started doodling and sketching to create a comic. As we explored different ideas, we came up with a slightly crazy story involving... you guessed it – CHOCOLATE!

It went something like this...

At a local fancy dress party, some aliens sneaked in and joined the party, but no one knew they were aliens because it was a fancy dress party - of course!

The aliens kidnapped all the people and took them to their planet Mars.

They contacted the chocolate factory Cadbury's, and asked for chocolate to be beamed across the universe in exchange for the earthlings. They received the chocolate and munched happily ever after.

OK so it wasn't the best-written or best drawn comic ever, but that didn't matter.

What's more, my mum didn't 'interfere' or try to dampen down my expectations. Instead she helped me post the comic to the wonderful people at Cadbury's and then we waited...

Can you guess what happened?

After a few days, we received a large box of chocolate. To be clear this was no ordinary sized box. Instead, this was a HUGE parcel bursting at the seams with bars and bars of my favourite chocolate.

I was nine. It was 1976, and paradise had arrived on the doormat!

Joanne and I were ecstatic.

And that was just the beginning...

Inspired by our success we created more stories about our favourite sweets. We had Jo Toffo, the coolest cowboy kid around, who often got into sticky situations. We also had the jelly babies who could bounce to super heights and transformed the colour of places, to name a few. We collated all our stories into a bigger comic. I decided the comic was worth a penny a read and so began charging my classmates 1p for the privilege of reading our stories!

What's more, because my friend's dad ran a sweet shop, I was able to trade reads for chocolate to make this a double success. I guess I had entrepreneurial instincts from an early age.

Looking back, the comic experience was hugely significant for me – even though I didn't appreciate it at the time.

I had proof that creativity could help me achieve the things I wanted and I had proof that anything was indeed possible. Mum was right.

More than that, the comic success boosted my self-esteem and gave me the confidence to explore more plans and ideas in the future. I'm grateful that my mum encouraged me to explore my ideas, discover opportunities and develop my plans. I'm certain this early experience laid the foundations for the other things I did as a child – and as an adult.

I often think back upon this early memory. I've even kept the comic and it still makes me smile.

It was only when I got the comic out again while writing this book that I realised the blue dudes that we use at The Creation Station now, look just like my original designs when I was nine. They're even the same turquoise colour. It goes to show you should never underestimate the power of imagination and where it can take you – even forty years after the time you first conceived an idea.

THE INVADERS
WE WILL SEE WHAT LIFE ON PLANET EARTH IS LIKE
THEY ENTERED THE HOUSE AND WAS WELCOMED BY A BIG CHEER
HORRAY!!
YOUR EARTHLING FOOD IS REALLY NICE
NOW I AM GOING TO JUDGE the competition PLEASE MAKE YOUR WAY TO THE NEXT ROOM AND STAND IN AN ORDERLY LINE
HERE'S THE LETTER HE GAVE ME. I'LL GO OVER TO CADBURYS NOW
A FEW WEEKS LATER THE INVADERS RECEIVED A BOX OF CHOCOLATE BARS
THANKYOU FOR YOUR OFFER. EVERY WEEK YOU WILL RECIEVE A BOX OF CHOCOLATE BARS
YOURS FAITHFULLY
IF ANYONE WONDERS WHY CADBURYS IS SUCH A BIG AND FAMOUS COMPANY THIS IS THE REASON AND AFTER READING THIS STORY YOU CAN GO AND TELL YOUR FRIENDS AND RELATIVES
Cadbury's DAIRY MILK
MILK CHOCOLATE
6th IS THE DUMMY
4th IS THE OXO CUBE
3rd IS THE WITCH AND GHOST
2nd IS THE PUNK ROCKER
AND FINALLY
1st IS OUR FRIENDS THE SPACEMEN
EAT THIS IT IS METTALIC A FAVOURITE FOOD.
AFTER 3 HOURS
GIVE THIS TO THE MANAGER
WE ARE THE OCCUPENTS OF PLANET PLUTO, AND WE WOULD LIKE TO MAKE AN AGREEMENT.
TO US EVERY TUESDAY WE WILL BEAM DOWN
FROM THE OCCUPENTS OF PLUTO

And now time for you

The human brain is always trying to protect us. It's why limiting thoughts and beliefs can stop us in our tracks when we start thinking big and creatively.

It's uncomfortable outside that comfort zone.

The problem with these thought processes is they can hold us back, stop us getting started, and crush dreams – even before we've had the chance to explore the possibilities.

> "What would you attempt to do if you knew you could not fail?"
>
> ***Robert H. Schuller***

Questions such as these inspire an entirely new train of thought. They open the door to new paths. They force us to think about how things could work out. It's the same process I used to turn an idea into chocolate.

As well as a great protector, the human brain is also an incredible tool for creative thinking. When you start to think about the things you want, your brain starts to generate solutions.

I invite you to spend some time thinking about what you would do if you couldn't fail. While thinking is the first step, you don't have to take big actions. Just grab a pen and some paper and start imagining.

And encourage your child to do the same.

Together, you can allow your imaginations to run away. You never know what tangible outcomes you may end up creating as a result.

Foundations for growth

As an adult, I enjoy reflecting on my experiences. What went well, what could have gone better and what I might do more of or differently next time. I feel you can learn a lot from looking back. It's surprising how the little things can make such an impact upon who you are and what you believe. After all, there's a lesson to be learned from every experience. I believe that's how we can grow as an individual – by learning from everything life throws at you. It's why reflection is a skill I've worked hard to develop.

And what I've discovered is that my past experiences and influences are responsible for making me the overall happy, creative, driven person I am today.

And I see how this approach has empowered me to try stuff and take risks – and put my creative ideas into action.

I would describe myself as positive and someone who likes to make the very best of the life we have. I find it a good coping strategy when things get tough, either emotionally, physically or mentally. I can see this outlook on life rubbing off on my children too. And I'm certain the happiness and fulfilment I feel stems from having a go at things outside my comfort zone and outlets to express my thoughts and feelings.

It's why creativity and self-expression are so valuable.

And it was my mum who sowed the seeds for this attitude in my life.

Mum has always had a big influence on me. I've already revealed how she inspired me to believe anything is possible – but that was just the start. Another key lesson I learnt from mum is to find joy in the smallest pleasures and see the inspiration that's all around us.

This is something that young children do all the time.

Being present in the moment.

It's often called mindfulness.

My mum worked full-time and with the demands of managing a house of seven she didn't have much cash either. But despite these challenges she always had a smile and still managed to give each of us quality time – and I treasure those memories (and try to do the same for my own kids).

For example, once a year, we all had our 'big treat' – a trip to Liverpool to buy school shoes.

When it was my turn to head into the bustling big city I was bursting with excitement. I don't remember much about the shoes, but I can vividly recall the trip's highlight – a visit to John Lewis.

I remember sitting with mum in the restaurant on the top floor enjoying the largest Knickerbocker Glory of my life - topped with lashings of chocolate sauce of course! I was sworn to secrecy. As far as my brothers and sisters were concerned we'd been out shopping for school shoes not fancy ice creams!

After our secret treat, mum and I explored the various departments. I remember being transfixed by the homeware in the basement.

In particular, I remember the beautiful cutlery – it looked like liquid silver to me. Bright and shiny, I couldn't believe that something so functional and an everyday item could be so beautiful.

In the end mum had to drag me away. Looking back, I know this early appreciation of the small things sparked my creativity. It's not unusual for me to see ideas and projects when I'm out and about because the unexpected or unremarkable can spark an idea or a thought in my imagination. And it's the same for many of us, when we take time to recognise it.

It's why I encourage my children to be curious about what's around them. To really look at what they see, hear, taste, smell, and feel. All this sensory information fuels our imagination and inspires our thinking. It's also enriching.

Mum also taught me to be independent and free thinking. Consideration and thoughtfulness was drilled into us, and with five siblings we learnt to value and respect each other's space, comments, and belongings. But my mum didn't want me to be reliant on approval from others when making choices. I think this desire to empower her children stemmed from her own experiences as a young woman.

Originally from Carlingford in Southern Ireland, and the youngest of three, mum found it a struggle to leave her home and move to Liverpool with my dad. She discovered that I'd told one of her friends I was going to stay home and look after her, she was keen to ensure I felt in no way obligated to do so – she wanted me to have the freedom to develop my own path and shape my own future.

To give me more choices, mum looked into boarding schools. When the conversation came up just after my thirteenth birthday, I was buzzing with the idea of going away to school. After all, the girls in the Malory Towers book by Enid Blyton, seemed to have a great time. When I think back to how my mum encouraged her youngest to leave home even when her other kids had just left home, and somehow found the money to finance the school, I am incredibly grateful.

As a mum now, I totally get putting your kids first and I see my role is to help my children blossom into the happy, thoughtful and healthy people they were born to be, to nurture their potential and equip them with a foundation of life skills to cope and thrive on their life journey.

Unsurprisingly, where I went to school, Our Lady's Convent School in Alnwick Northumberland wasn't quite Malory Towers. As the newcomer in a school with established classmates I quickly learnt to stand on my own two feet. For sure there were days when I missed home and struggled with my identity, but overall I coped because mum filled me with self-reliance, confidence, and belief in myself.

"Two roads diverged in a wood, and I took the one less travelled by, and that has made all the difference."

Robert Frost – The Road Not Taken
(2)

As you know, confidence is hugely important for children – and adults.

In the absence of self-belief we can struggle to have faith in ourselves. We can doubt our thoughts, creations, and our imagination, meaning our feelings, stories, and brilliant ideas stay locked in our head.

My mum helped ensure that didn't happen to me. Instead, I felt safe enough to express freely my creative thoughts and ideas.

These positive experiences also enriched my mind and inspired my thinking. As a result, from a very young age I've always been hungry to try new things and explore new places. I enjoyed stepping out of my comfort zone so that I could discover and live life.

It was this open mind, which made me excited to read Anita Roddick's autobiography when I was given it as a gift on my thirteenth birthday. Although I was familiar with The Body Shop, I hadn't heard of its founder. But her book quickly had me hooked. I was fascinated by Anita's philosophy. Her ability to communicate her ideas and make a difference to the whole beauty industry through her passion and beliefs was inspirational.

And while I had no aspirations to create a company at this point, as a kid I didn't really know what I wanted to be, the idea that a business could make a tangible difference and not just sell products really resonated. In fact, I believe Anita Roddick's story is one of the reasons why The Creation Station came about and has its core purpose to make a positive difference.

And now time for you

Looking back, I can see how my childhood experiences created the framework and motivation for what I do in my work and how I raise my children. Everything from losing my dad, to boarding school, to turning doodles into chocolate has led to the person and mother I am today.

It will be the same for you too...

If you look back, you'll discover stand out childhood experiences that have influenced your life and therefore how you interact with your children too. Some of these experiences will be empowering whereas others may be more negative.

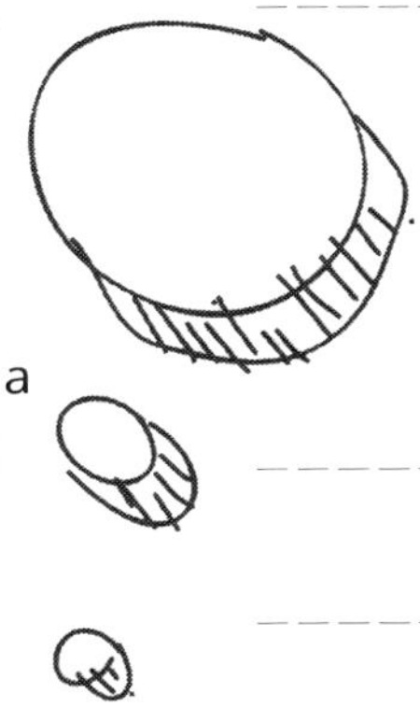

So, use this space to recall these memories and explore how they've influenced you and if you are a parent, your parenting. What can you learn? What can you do more of? What do you want to phase out?

Reflection is a critical skill to develop (and to teach our children). As we try to raise happy, healthy, creative children you'll often find it starts with you.

Hard decisions and choosing life

As the youngest of six, I truly was 'the baby'. My older brothers and sisters were all born within a period of five years – Hugh, Paul, Emily, George and Fran and then there was a four-year gap before I came along.

That said, being the youngest did have its advantages!

It's true. You can't control the situation you're born into. And yes it was hard – especially after dad died. It was tough on my siblings as everyone stepped up to help manage the household and the multitude of tasks that are involved in running a home for seven. I'm still very grateful to them for all their love and enabling me to have a carefree and fun childhood.

I'm a firm believer that you have to make the most of what you've got. It's easy to blame outside circumstances when things go wrong, but it's far better to grasp the opportunities and resources you do have – and then use those to make things happen for you.

> "The best way to predict your future is to create it."
>
> ***Abraham Lincoln***

This was another lesson that mum sowed the seeds of.

You see, she understood this concept too. For example, because I was the baby and Fran, who was four years older than me was about to start school, mum was concerned I wouldn't have children of my own age to play with. She set about fixing this by setting up a local playgroup. Looking back, this idea was forward thinking. Remember, it was the late '60s and playgroups were just emerging as an idea.

It just goes to show what you're able to create when you have a clear goal and the motivation to do what it takes – another lesson mum taught me.

We didn't have much extended family, but it was always an adventure to meet up with my Uncle Frank and Aunty Ruth and my six cousins, Stephen, Tony, Rachel, Mary, Liz ad Michael. Their Granny Dolly was also so kind and when we went around she would stretch up and remove her special tin and allow us to choose from so many yummy things. In fact, this experience stuck in my mind so much that when I came across a lovely Benjamin Rabbit tin when my boys were small, I had to buy it. Even now, years later it still lives on a top shelf. However, with three strapping boys in the house now, it's usually empty. I've since found a different 'safe' place to keep my little stash of chocolate!

The only grandparent I was ever fortunate to meet was my Grandpa Hugh, my mum's dad who we saw when we went over to Carlingford. My mum's family owned P.J. O'Hare's bar, grocery and sweet shop, so it was always fun to go and visit.

The summer after my dad died I headed over there with Fran and George, for the whole summer. We were made so welcome by our aunts and uncles and lovely cousins, Peter, Patricia and Mary. I had my first experience of water skiing and sailing and even won the Omeath regatta with my talented cousin, Peter. Carlingford is at the foot of the Mountains of Mourne and it was here I can safely say I fell in love with beautiful countryside and outdoor activities.

My mum loved being around kids – I guess it's why she had six of us! And she'd always wanted to work with children. In 1985, mum finally followed her passion and secured a job as Head of Childcare in Kingston Upon Thames. Our family home in Bootle, Liverpool was on the market but hadn't sold so, she took out a bridging loan and headed off to Kingston where she didn't know a soul. On reflection she'd say it was one of the best decisions she made and she's not quite sure how she found the courage to do it – but she's very pleased she did.

At the time I'd just completed my O-Levels and after two years at boarding school in Alnwick Northumberland, I felt I was missing out on normal, family life. I wanted a dose of reality. I moved to

Kingston upon Thames with mum, joined the local Tudor school to start my A-Levels, and quickly made some brilliant friends.

Unfortunately or fortunately – depending on your perspective, I enjoyed my 'dose of reality' a little bit too much!

You see, I LOVED my newfound freedom and friends in sixth form, but perhaps not surprisingly I didn't do as well in my A-Levels as I thought I would. When it was time to leave school, like many teenagers, I didn't know what to do next. It was a strange feeling to have this choice to make and to be so unsure of what to do next for the best.

Mum helped out again... she said to me, "Sarah, people always have to eat."

Fran was studying for a degree in nutrition and catering at Huddersfield Polytechnic, now university. Catering wasn't really 'my thing', but with nothing else catching my attention it seemed like a 'sensible' choice – especially because there was a clear career progression and something with a lot of jobs available.

We all have times in our lives when the route to take is unclear and sometimes the practical choice is the right one to take. Hindsight is a wonderful thing, but we have to make decisions with the information we have at the time. I've found this a helpful way to cope with decisions that haven't always gone to plan. Even some of the most difficult experiences can have surprising outcomes that you can take from it. You learn from everything you do and as you learn more, so you grow.

In September 1985, I got on a coach to Huddersfield to start my new venture doing a BSc in Catering and Applied Nutrition at Huddersfield Poly. As I'd already been to boarding school I was 'OK' with the idea of living away from home again and I was looking forward to getting stuck into the student lifestyle.

I remember my first day – I walked down a very long hill and followed all the other young people towards the big registration hall. The large hall had letters hanging from the ceiling. My surname back then was Long, so I queued up under the large 'L'. When I reached the desk I explained I was here to enrol. The lady behind the counter gave me a rather funny look. "This is the dole office luv, the poly is down the road."

Whoops! The day could only get better!

I quickly settled into my new life at Huddersfield. There was lots to do and lots to learn. I was just your typical student making the most of the freedoms and opportunities that students have.

Like many students, I worked alongside studying. I worked in a number of bars and in the staff bar. Over the years I was there, my great friend Wendy and I were promoted to the heady heights of managing the staff bar on many late nights. It was great fun getting to know the staff and we did have our fair share of lock-ins and singalongs with the piano.

I was fortunate that Fran was already at Huddersfield and where she lived was conveniently on the route home to my shared student house. It would have been rude not to pop in on my way home. I don't recall doing this intentionally, but apparently I would always pop in at teatime, where I would be kindly offered a bowl of something tasty to eat. This was really handy because my first year's student grant (yes we really did get paid to go to college then) was late. I recall my grant finally arrived a week before the end of the first term. I'd never had so much money before, so I did the most logical thing I could think of. I went out and bought a really cool black leather jacket! Fran for some reason has never let me forget my 'random' popping in at teatime visits.

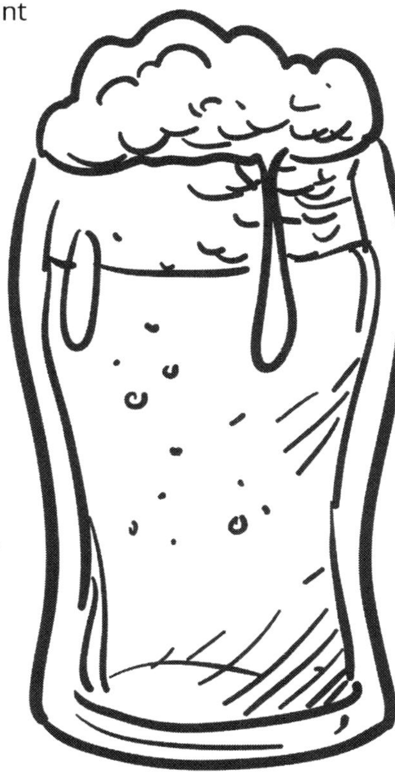

One of the great things about being a student is the long summer holidays, so Wendy and I decided to save up and buy an Interrail pass to travel around Europe. With rucksack, small cooking stove, and a map of Europe we set off from Waterloo Station to go exploring.

My biggest memory of this adventure was the fact that we stayed on the train every night. Even if we arrived at a city we liked, we would still travel seven hours overnight to another city on the train, spend the day in a different city, then return back the next day to spend some more time in the place we liked. We were fortunate to see a wealth of sights. We walked the stunning gorge of Samaria in Crete – in flip-flops, which seriously isn't the way to do it! We got sunburnt swimming in a lake somewhere in Sweden, we travelled around Budapest on a tiny train run by children, and we met an array of curious and interesting people. We ended up in Greece, with no money so we slept on the beach – the tan was good and we were both delighted to get back home!

My second year at Huddersfield Poly started as normal, until tragedy struck my family again when my beloved brother Paul died.

He was a diver with the Royal Navy Reserves and was diving one weekend when there was an accident. I don't know if you've ever lost someone you love, but amongst the many feelings was my broken heart. I remember the overwhelming sadness of missing someone who made me laugh a lot and made me feel special. After losing my dad, the pain was unbearable. It hit all of us hard and threw us into turmoil.

Now that I'm a mother myself, I don't know how my mum coped. She had to deal with every parent's worst nightmare. But she was so strong and as a family we were so supportive of each other.

I'd already learned that life is short and finite after dad died; Paul's death was a cruel reminder. His death was a huge shock that taught me how precious life and time is. Alongside my grief, I remember feeling overwhelmed by an acute awareness of the need to make the most of every day.

I therefore had to deal with a dilemma.

You see, before Paul died I'd been busy making plans to travel to Israel and work on a Kibbutz for the summer. Those boarding school years had made me comfortable with the idea of exploring different places and I was excited about experiencing a foreign country and a new way of life.

But now that Paul had died I was no longer clear on the right thing to do. I was due to leave just five weeks later and it felt too soon.

Part of me felt I should stay at home so I could be close to mum and my brothers and sisters. I knew I'd feel safe if I did that.

But another part of me still wanted to get out there and experience all life had to offer.

I mulled over the decision – a lot – until I knew what the right decision was. I had to choose to live my life.

Paul had an adventurous spirit too and I knew he would have

encouraged me to go to Israel. But still it wasn't easy. Like many others, I've endured tough times in my life, but waving goodbye to mum as the coach pulled away from Sheffield station in the summer of 1987 was one of the hardest things I've faced.

But I trusted my instincts and knew my choice had been the right one.

Experiencing life on a Kibbutz was amazing and the communal lifestyle turned out to be exactly what I needed. The experience was very healing. It was also quite strange. You see, we lived in little concrete bunkhouses, which got so hot because the temperatures soared to 45^{0}C.

If you aren't familiar with a Kibbutz, it's a voluntary, democratic community in Israel where people live and work together. One of the jobs I had to do was prepare breakfast. This involved getting up at 5am to unlock and open up the large kitchen.

Every morning I'd start my day standing at a sink washing vegetables and watching the most incredible sunrise. One morning

I was lost in daydreams when I heard the kitchen manager shout out to me, “Quick Sarah give me a kiss.”

I was a little surprised and turned around and said “Pardon!”

She was coming towards me with her arms outstretched and started shouting, “I need a kiss now!”

I put my arms up and said no, no way.

She reached out and grabbed the front of my apron and removed the keys. “Next time,” she said, “Remember to hang the kiss up on the hook!”

Phew! Talk about the difficulty that can arise when communicating!

After three weeks my work changed and I was rota’d to work in the wheel factory. Here I assembled what seemed like one thousand wheels a day. It was a very repetitive job but at the same time quite relaxing.

On a Monday someone baked a cake and everyone took turns cleaning the loos; even the MD of the business. It was a very collaborative way of working with a lovely atmosphere.

I’d typically work six hours and with an early start sometimes finished work at 11am. This meant I had the whole day to potter, chat with other people working there or ‘Kibbutzniks’ as we were called.

I became good friends with a couple of guys Ross and Chris. I have to say Ross did look like Jesus, even down to the sandals and was a very caring guy. I’m not sure if this was just because I’d visited Jerusalem and the idea was in my head, but he was a pretty cool laid-back guy, who worked in the film industry in New York. We did go to a Bob Dylan concert in Tel Aviv together, which was so laid-back and chilled I fell asleep and missed the last bus.

Chris was in his early twenties. He was quite quiet, but when you chatted with him his stories were incredible. I don't recall all the details, but if I share with you what I took away from his overall stories, I hope you'll see why he made a lasting impression.

Chris had been travelling for quite a few years and during this time he'd support himself by working in the countries he visited.

He decided to get work as a chef, but he didn't want to be a general chef. Instead, he wanted to specialise and learn a new skill. He decided to focus on learning macrobiotic cookery.

Macrobiotics is a way of eating based on ideas about types of food drawn from Zen Buddhism. The diet attempts to balance the yin and yang of food and cookware, reduce animal products, eat seasonal food grown locally, and eat in moderation.

This was back in the 1980s so you can see the essence is still very relevant today.

So, back to the story...

He worked every hour he could and over a few years soon mastered the art. He got well known and ended up with his own TV show.

He did that for a while and then he decided he wanted to do something else. So he trained to be a masseur.

He committed the time and practice to mastering the skill, and ended up being the masseur for the royal household in somewhere like Sudan.

I was totally in awe that you could choose a path you wanted to take and with passion and commitment excel in what you put your energy and focus into.

It made me realise:

"Whatever you do, be the best that you can."

After my five weeks on the Kibbutz I travelled down to the Dead Sea in the back of an open-air truck.

The song playing was Black's 'Wonderful life'. It made me think of Paul and I felt so grateful for the opportunities I was so fortunate to have. I continued to travel down to Egypt and into the Sahara Desert.

Here was I, experiencing different cultures, making new friends and learning about so many different perspectives. It was indeed a wonderful life and one that I believe is an outcome of how you view and choose life.

One memorable occasion I booked a tour to spend the night in the Sahara Desert with some travelling nomads and a friend Alison, that I'd met on the Kibbutz. I have never seen such a HUGE star-studded sparkly sky. It was so vast and clear and so silent.

I'd been warned about the wild dogs and we had one of the local nomads on guard, as we were literally in a sleeping bag on the desert sand.

I heard a deep low, growling noise, and it seemed to be getting louder and louder. I had to choose between hiding in my sleeping bag or being prepared to roar back. I decided it would be better to prepare myself, so I peeped out of my bag listening for the direction of the sounds.

It was then I realised that my friend Alison... had just started a new habit... snoring!

It ruined the silent, calmest of all sparkly nights, but it was nevertheless, a very memorable occasion.

As a result, 30 years later these experiences still remain close to my heart. In fact, to this day I still feel privileged that I experienced, shared and was part of a Kibbutzim community.

When it was over I felt ready to return to the UK and continue my studies at Huddersfield – with one difference...

After everything that had happened, I was ready to discover the things I really wanted to do with my life.

And surprisingly it didn't take long...

It was the late '80s and the mass media coverage of the devastating famine in Ethiopia was at its peak. Live Aid was on the TV and like many others, I was moved by the tragic images of helpless children suffering with malnutrition. I felt drawn to Africa.

I wanted to go and do something to help.

At this stage what exactly I would do I didn't know, but where there's a will, there's a way.

I've found intuition to be a powerful player in my life – as is the power of intention. Like my decision to go to the Kibbutz, I was drawn to go to Africa. And just like the comic that I turned into chocolate, I believed I'd find a way to make an African trip possible.

Then Emily, my eldest sister, told me about Operation Raleigh – this is now called Raleigh International – and instantly, I knew it was going to be the route for me to be able to volunteer in Africa.

It was time to grab life.

Emily explained that Operation Raleigh had a selection weekend and if chosen there were different locations you could go to.

I knew this was the right opportunity for me. In fact, I was so inspired that I booked myself onto the very next selection weekend that had availability – just two days after my finals.

It felt brilliant to discover something that sparked my interest after four years of studying catering, which although had been good, didn't really click with me. In hindsight, Operation Raleigh was the start of getting my life back on track because it was my choice based on what sparked my interest.

If you've heard of Operation Raleigh you'll know it's physically demanding and challenging. With limited spaces and lots of interest a place is far from guaranteed. I knew it would be tough and as the selection date drew nearer I realised just how much I wanted a place on the expedition.

Spurred on by the loss of my brother, the understanding that time passes too quickly, and the harsh reality that uncertainty is always around the corner, I decided to make the most of this chance.

And this drive changed my thinking and my approach...

I decided to do everything I possibly could to secure my space. Not just my best.

That way I knew if I did fail, and failure was an option, I could be disappointed, but not regretful. If I did everything I could, I'd know in my heart that I couldn't have done any more and if I didn't achieve my goal of getting on, at least I would know I couldn't have done any more.

It's an approach and an attitude that I've used many times since.

With a focused goal, I made changes to my lifestyle to boost my chance of getting a place.

I swapped late student nights for sleep so I could run in the mornings. I knew fitness and stamina would increase my chances so this new routine was critical – even though it was tough. I was a terrible runner, but I stuck at it. There were some days I had to lie down for a 'power nap' halfway around my route! It was only when some bloke prodded me to see if I was still alive that I put a stop to my mid-run sleeps.

Despite my preparation, when the selection weekend arrived it was tougher than I expected. It was like an SAS survival TV programme; relentless, muddy, and very exhausting!

By the end of it I was covered in bruises and could hardly walk, but I survived. I know you're not supposed to shout encouragement from the back, but it was the only way I could cope and I knew I'd done my best.

Now it was just a waiting game – and having just finished my finals after a four-year degree I was enjoying the freedom of not having to study every spare moment I had and I had lots of cool stuff booked in.

With my new freedom over my time, I had some things I wanted to crack on with. First up was my driving test – the Monday after the selection weekend. I didn't pass, because frustratingly I couldn't perform the reverse around the corner manoeuvre, despite being able to do it in practice. Unbeknown to me I'd broken my wrist on my right hand, during the Raleigh selection weekend. I thought it was a bit sore but as the whole of me was sore from the full-on physical weekend I hadn't given it any special attention.

A quick dash to the hospital left me with a big cast, and then two days later I flew out to Canada for a two-month working holiday with my wonderful friend, Wendy. I loved hanging out with her and she was and is an awesome mate. We were perfect travelling and side-kick buddies!

My brother George had moved to Canada in the mid '80s and met and married a wonderful Canadian called Janice. I was very fortunate that they were happy to invite Wendy and I over to stay and very kindly use their place as a base. This was so generous and kind of them. It was a wonderful way to get to know my new sister-in-law and I'm pleased that we have remained firm friends ever since. Their three kids, Jordan, Rachel and Gabe are great fun and are good friends with ours and although it's the other side of the world, Skype and FaceTime make the distances small.

Back in 1989, I hadn't planned for my right arm to be in a cast, but it didn't stop me going to Canada and actually it turned out to have its benefits. You see, I got the 'pleasant' waitressing jobs at the Waffle House restaurant in Toronto, whilst Wendy had to work in the very hot and shouty kitchen.

Wendy and I worked really hard – in fact we took on four jobs. We were at the Waffle House during the day, Dunkin Donuts in the evenings, and then we sold newspaper subscriptions for two competing newspapers at the weekends.

We had a good routine going. On Friday nights we would sell subscriptions for the Toronto Star, then when we spoke to people who told us exactly what they thought of that paper, and that they only ever read the Toronto Sun, we'd ask them if they would be interested in a special offer on that subscription instead. If they said yep, we would give them a call on Saturday evening at our other job… you guessed, selling subscriptions for the other paper. I don't think this would be legal now, but back then we weren't aware of any rules we were breaking and in fact we had some of the best sales figures in the call centre.

It was pretty full on working, but it was great fun and we met lots of very different and interesting people. We ate for free in the waffle house and donut shop and needless to say grew in not just experience but in waistband size too. The working holiday was a great experience and all our hard work paid off. We put all our tips in a bucket so we could see the dollars literally growing every day. We earned enough cash to fund an unforgettable tour around America from New York to New Orleans and down to Mexico.

One memory that jumps out is our arrival in New York. My friend Ross, who I'd met on the Kibbutz, lived on Long Island so he met Wendy and I at the airport. Ross had organised a chauffeur driven stretch Limo, to show us around New York. the car came with a very well stocked bar.

We saw all the sights, emptied the bar, and arrived at Ross's home in the early hours. I still have visions of Wendy and I stumbling out of the Limo like Patsy and Edina in a scene from Ab Fab. Wendy had blonde curly hair so obviously she was Patsy!

We also met up with my friend Julie in California who I'd been at sixth form with. We visited the Grand Canyon and traversed down through seven of the world's climates as we approached the green winding Colorado river at the bottom of the incredible canyon. We cycled round New Orleans, got sunburnt in San Diego where we used aloe plants from the beach to soothe our skin, and enjoyed playing in Disneyland in torrential rain with no queues. It was amazing. We chatted, ate and laughed our way around the length and breadth of the States.

The time passed too quickly though and before we knew it, it was time to waddle home – a stone and a half heavier – to collect our degrees in Catering and Nutrition!

Looking back, the experiences from my student days helped shape my attitude and approach to life in adulthood. I started at Huddersfield with no clear idea of what I wanted to do, but left with a clear understanding that I would grab life and do the things I loved.

After all, life is too short to play safe and stick to doing the things that don't make you smile.

I'd also learnt the power of decision-making. I know my life would have turned out differently if I'd made different choices. For example, if I'd let a broken arm stop me going to Canada, or if I'd half-heartedly gone after the Raleigh place...

Some decisions were easy and others were incredibly tough, but most importantly I chose what I felt was right for me. And I was able to do that because of the independence, self-belief, and self-reliance my childhood had given me.

I had the courage to step out of my comfort zone and choose my own path. And my life has been enriched as a result.

> "When someone makes a decision, he is really diving into a strong current that will carry him to places he never dreamed of when he first made the decision."
>
> ***Paul Coelho, The Alchemist***
> (3)

And now time for you

Life happens – and unless we stay aware, it's easy to drift and end up on autopilot arriving at a destination that's not of our choosing. In the blink of an eye, weeks, months, even years can pass and great opportunities can be missed.

Decisions can alter and affect the journey of our life too.

Remember. To decide to do nothing is still a decision. That's why empowering children to make their own choices is a skill that can equip them for future success, happiness, and fulfilment. I know how different my life felt when I started to do the things that were more based on how I felt and my gut instinct.

Think back to the key decisions you've made in your life and what impact upon they have had. Write down some areas in your life where you want to make some decisions and start to weigh up the impact upon the different options available to you.

If you have children, give them opportunities to make their own choices and help them understand and accept that their decisions have effects and consequences.

T-shirts designed and sold to raise funds for my Operation Raleigh expedition.

Out in Africa with Operation Raleigh

Sept 1990 - May 1991

My student days were over, so when I arrived back from my working holiday and American road trip, I had to think about work.

Fortunately, within days of returning to England, I was offered a job as a catering manager in London with a company that I'd worked with on placement. It was July 1989.

I was soon managing a team and helping with the foodservice for a range of different contracts including The Treasury, The Old Bailey, The BBC, merchant banks, and universities. It was fascinating seeing behind the scenes of these incredible institutions. But that wasn't all...

I was elated to discover I'd been offered a place on the three-month Operation Raleigh expedition to Zimbabwe starting in September 1990. All the effort and commitment had paid off.

There was just one stumbling block... I had to raise £2,500.

As you can imagine, this was a serious amount of cash – especially for a graduate in her first job, but I was focused and determined. I had clarity and that made me energised. Somehow clarity un-bundles all the confusion and I was committed to do whatever it takes.

While others were relying on sponsorships, I wanted more control. I had an idea. I took out a £1,200 bank loan and invested in 1000 printed

T-shirts bearing a mural I'd recently designed and painted at Charing Cross station.

It was a risk taking a loan. There was no guarantee I'd get the return, but I was determined to give it a try. After all, I believe if you want something, you have to put everything in and focus on the one thing to give yourself the best chance of making it work. I was prepared to do that.

I was proud of the 30-foot mural I'd created on Villiers Street at Charing Cross Station. It was bold and eye-catching and I believed the design on a T-shirt would sell well.

I put myself right out there to sell one thousand T-shirts. For example, I stood by the mural and sold T-shirts to passers-by. I also had a stall at Camden Market, and of course lots of supportive family, friends, and work colleagues – as well as many kind strangers! In addition to the T-shirts, I also went around pubs selling chocolate. I had to give up my nights out, but I had a bigger purpose and the sacrifice was worth it!

I also did a sponsored walk – the three tallest peaks in the UK... Ben Nevis, Scafell Pike and Snowden. I hadn't quite appreciated how much it would take out of me, I didn't even take the Monday off. Sometimes ignorance really isn't bliss! I was running the catering at Mercury Communications at King's Cross station at the time and I used to cycle in from Wood Green. But I got the tube in that Monday and could hardly walk down the steps to the underground. It was a tough day in the kitchen on that occasion, I can tell you.

However, my efforts and investment paid off and soon I had enough cash to fund my expedition place. I was going to Zimbabwe and I was absolutely over the moon!

The year or so between finding out I had a place and leaving for the trip passed quickly. And then the big day arrived. It was September 1990 and I was living in a flat in Finsbury Park, North London. I'd packed my rucksack and was all ready to leave for the airport the following day. The only problem was that every time I looked at my packed rucksack, I felt really really sick and had to keep rushing to the toilet.

I was scared to be going on this big adventure. I didn't know anyone and I didn't know how long I'd be away for. I had to hide my bag because it was a harsh reminder of the cold reality of what I was about to do.

The fear was terrifying, but my intuition reassured me that I was doing the right thing. Part of me wanted to stay, but a bigger part of me wanted to get on that plane. After all, I'd worked so hard for this moment – it had been a big achievement to secure a place. I couldn't (and wouldn't) back out now.

The next day, I got to the airport only to discover that my flight was delayed for eight hours. I remember laughing to myself and thinking, "Sarah you got all worried and worked up about sitting in an airport all day."

It was then when I realised that the thought of something is often far worse than the reality itself. And worrying doesn't help an awful lot.

Africa turned out to be a watershed moment for me.

I met fantastic people in Africa – locals as well as my expedition pals – in particular, Nicky and Kerry who remain two of my closest friends to this day. However, my Operation Raleigh experience didn't go quite as I expected.

During the first two weeks we headed out for a three-day, white-water rafting expedition down the Zambezi, starting at the foot of Victoria Falls. I was so excited.

Unfortunately, on the morning of day one, the boat bounced like crazy on the huge white-water waves, and crashed into the craggy boulders. Somehow all eight of us in the boat managed to hang on, but I landed awkwardly on my left knee. Worse still, I managed to jar and twist my knee on one of the huge river boulders under the boat. In fact, it was so twisted I thought it had actually twisted right off. I remember looking down expecting to see my leg floating next to me. Thankfully it was still attached.

My knee quickly swelled to the size of a balloon and turned an odd colour. I later found out I'd torn my cartilage. But sitting in the inflatable boat all I felt was utter devastation - despite the excruciating pain. After all that effort to get me here, I'd become injured within the first few days.

What impact would this have upon my trip?

But then I realised there was a much more immediate concern. You see, there was no easy way for me to be taken out of the area. I had to stay on the boat for another two and a half days.

It was terrifying...

White-water rafting is very unpredictable. You need to stay alert – and preferably remain in the boat. If the boat flips, you don't want to get stuck underneath or sucked into a whirlpool. If you do, you have to kick your legs pretty hard to get back to the surface.

As you can imagine, my badly swollen knee limited my ability to do that. My brother, Paul was also vividly in my mind too. You'll remember he'd drowned just two years previously. I couldn't bear the thought of putting my mum or my family through that grief again.

Unsurprisingly, I faced a tense few days as I fiercely gripped the boat with all my energy. You could say it was a true white-knuckle white-water rafting experience.

And to top it off, night times weren't any more relaxed either. We had to sleep on the side of the river at least eight feet from the riverbanks. That way we wouldn't be easy prey for the crocodiles that made the Zambezi their home. I know, it sounds like something from a movie and it did feel surreal at times.

I was scared. But I knew how I would cope would be down to the way I approached the situation.

I used my creative thinking to help calm my worried mind.

I listened to our white-water rafting expert share stories of the river god – Nyami Nyami, and saw incredible etchings of the river god on the valley walls. It made me remember what a privilege it was to be in this stunningly green and abundant place, inaccessible in any other way. I asked the river god to transport me and my friends safely along their beautiful and powerful river.

I learnt to seek out the positive and find gratitude. Rather than seeing the river as something to be feared, I focussed on respecting the river, valuing its beauty and power, and celebrating all those who had passed this way before.

When it was all over I realised just how much the experience of creative thinking sparked and strengthened my coping strategies and problem-solving techniques.

Needless to say, we all survived the three-day white-water raft. As we trekked (and in my case hopped) to the pick-up point I recall nipping behind a large bush for a quick loo break. I soon realised we were no longer in no-man's land, when I heard the 'toot toot' of a large army truck driving just behind me. I was so surprised I quickly turned around, lost my balance on my rather wobbly leg and fell backwards.

Yep I was squatting on the side of a road – embarrassed doesn't even touch it. Oh well, I'm sure I gave them a laugh!

Out of the boat and back on dry land I had my knee checked out and discovered I had torn my cartilage. I had three options. One, to have it operated on asap. Two, to go home and have it operated on, or three to carry on with crutches and painkillers and get it fixed after the expedition.

Now, it probably doesn't come as any surprise that I took the third option of crutches and painkillers and wobbled about for the next three months.

We were building a vehicle workshop in Mana Pools, which meant heavy lifting and lots of manual work, so I offered to stay at the camp and do the catering. Not quite my plan for my African adventure, but it was a way of contributing to the team.

Which when I think back about this it wasn't the most restful activity I could have chosen. It involved heading out in the morning finding and lugging firewood, carrying supplies, lifting heavy saucepans and feeding up to twenty-five people at a time. Then when everyone went off to work on the vehicle workshop I'd do the washing up. Not the most relaxing or easy job on the camp, but it was the one thing I could just about do.

The rest of the team were out all day, I spent a fair bit of time by myself. With a bit of creative thinking I found plenty to occupy my time.

Do you remember the horrible shiny toilet tissue paper you sometimes get in school? Well this was part of the Raleigh rations and we had lots of it. So, I came up with a much more interesting way to use it. I'd brought my felt pens, so I got these out and decorated hundreds of sheets of loo paper. I scrunched it up and tied them together into bunches of three and tied them to the tree branches. I also created menus for the food I'd prepared and some tantalising pre-menu signs and attached them to the trees so when everyone came back from their day's work they would get a sense of anticipation for the food that awaited them.

I loved decorating the camp and I began to appreciate how creative activities could positively change the atmosphere, lift the spirits, and alter how people felt.

To be honest, with the rations we had, you had to be quite creative to make anything halfway tasty. With the help of some of the guys in the group we built an underground oven. We dug a hole, made a fire and used a metal tray. We could now slow cook the rations and we even managed to make and bake some pizzas.

When everyone had gone off to work, I didn't see anyone until they returned later in the afternoon. One afternoon, I'd done all the jobs so decided to have an afternoon of naked drawing.

Not me drawing naked people or animals, but me just stripping off and drawing some of the landscapes.

I have no idea what possessed me to do this, but anyway there I was, getting into my sketches when I heard the crack of some branches behind me. It sounded like a gunshot and my fear was accentuated by the fact that I was starkers – apart from a rather grubby bandage on my knee. I turned around to find a baboon with a bottle of deodorant.

I'm not kidding, he or she had found the bottle lying around and come for a little explore.

It did put an end to my naked drawing, which to be honest was probably a good thing. It also explained why so many people had complained about losing some of their stuff. We soon expected to see a sweet-smelling baboon wearing socks, sunglasses, and a bra come join us in camp.

It turned out this cheeky little baboon would often pop over in the afternoon for a little browse.

Being on crutches meant I wasn't as mobile as I would have liked. Thankfully there was a wheelbarrow at camp. I got pushed around in this quite a bit. Nicky and Kerry were brilliant at pushing me along so I got out of the camp. One early evening we went for a wander when suddenly this enormous bull elephant appeared out of nowhere, her giant ears outstretched, which if you're not familiar with the general behaviour traits of African elephants, means they are about to charge... right at you.

So, the only thing we could do was to RUN.

I've no idea how I did it but tipped myself out of the wheelbarrow and legged it.

The doctor did say when I eventually got my knee fixed that he was surprised how much worse it had become. I wonder why.

While in Africa we worked on another project too – building a village school in Rusape. Again, I couldn't help with the building work, but I did turn my hand to creating a mural on the wall with some friends and the locals. We burnt wood to create charcoal to create the design. The locals made some scaffolding from tree trunks and rope. I was nervous the first time I climbed to the top – not wanting to damage my other knee or anything else. But it was fine and within seven days we created a mural to celebrate the relationship of Raleigh with the school.

It felt good to be doing this creative work and contributing to the team.

My thinking was changing too...

Initially, I'd wanted to go to Africa to do something to help with the famine. I'd imagined that once in Africa, I'd find ways that I could use my skills in catering and nutritional knowledge to somehow help. But I soon became aware that even with a degree in nutrition I didn't even know what questions to ask, let alone offer any tangible solutions or answers.

That said, my desire to help and make a difference was just as strong – I simply needed to find a different way that was more aligned with my skills and expertise.

And creativity became the key...

With my injured knee came the opportunity to explore my creative ideas around the camp. As a result, I began to understand the wider impact upon creative thinking – on problem-solving and wellbeing.

The dots began to connect:

- How I'd used creativity to solve my childhood chocolate problem
- How creativity funded my expedition to Africa
- How a creative approach to thinking helped me face my fears and overcome challenges

Then, on 2nd December 1998 whilst sitting on the dusty ground with my crutches propped up under a Jacaranda tree, I was asked if I would help set up and run a women's arts and crafts rural business development programme.

It sounded like the absolute perfect role for me. I knew I could make a difference with creativity. It's where I'd felt most alive for so long – from my chocolate focussed comic, to the Charing Cross mural, and everything in between, I felt at my happiest and most fulfilled when I allowed my creativity to take over.

Even though I would have loved the role, I felt it wasn't right for me at that moment in time. I trusted my intuition. Instinctively, I knew I still had work to do before I could inspire creativity in others, or help them run a business. I needed to work on my own creativity and learn more about running a business first.

But what to do next?

Whilst I'd enjoyed the challenges of catering management, my Operation Raleigh experience had intensified my desire to do something I loved. Looking back, I'd sensed for a long time that my passion for creativity and business would somehow come together, I just didn't know how - yet... I needed to have an operation on my knee. I could go home and have it done, but as I'd been so looking forward to coming to Africa it seemed a shame to go back to the UK so soon. To help make my decision, I spoke with a number of people to weigh up the pros, cons, and risks of staying. In the end I decided to stay, have the operation in the capital Harare, and take it easy for a while afterwards.

I was quite scared and really low in the hospital. However a few others were staying on from the expedition, and we had all become great friends and they were very lovely and came to visit me.

Although it was a tough decision to stay, I'm so glad that I did. One of the highlights of my extended stay was inviting my mum over. We spent two weeks travelling round Zimbabwe together. We shared a truly magical time. Although I don't think she was so keen on the day we found a deadly Boomslang snake lurking in the room of our little rondavel house. Our visitor was large and venomous. It was terrifying. Luckily, I'd learnt a little bit about jungle survival and managed to remove the snake from the room and contact the local snake expert. Talk about getting myself out of there.

I also travelled for six months with my new friend Kerry. Together we did some voluntary work. The amazing sights, sounds, and hospitality of many warm-spirited and kind people were memorable and unforgettable.

To this day, my African adventure remains one of my favourite memories. I can't believe all the incredible things I experienced and the warmth and kindness I received from the people I met.

And how significant it was for what came next...

And now time for you

In the last chapter I talked about the importance of decision-making. Often fear, pressure, the effort involved – even not wanting to stand out from the crowd can affect the choices we make.

Being aware of the factors that influence our choices can help us make better-informed decisions. It can prevent us from compromising or settling for something that wasn't our first choice. Instead, we can begin to explore, identify, and understand what we truly seek.

As a result, it can be powerful to reflect back on things that you wanted and think about the thinking, attitude, and behaviours that influenced your final choice. In addition, it can bring to you awareness of the times when you have overcome challenges and your self-confidence has been boosted.

Remember, all these experiences help to determine what you will do in the future – as well as influencing what you teach your children – either consciously or subconsciously.

Use this space to make a note of your ideas.

A different path

By now, I knew I didn't want a long-term future in catering. Perhaps the signs had been there all along.

My creative skills did extend into the kitchen, but not necessarily with the best results. For example, I loved making fudge – and was often delighting my siblings with my culinary masterpieces. However, these home-made treats weren't always the expected texture or colour.

I vividly recall the time when Emily's boyfriend said he'd like to try my new batch of fudge. He was asked whether he'd like one spoon or two. I have to say I think the addition of green food colouring was a creative step too far. The final result looked too much like washing-up liquid.

Looking back, this could have been an early warning signal that perhaps a career in catering wasn't going to be the most fulfilling career path for me.

However, I felt fortunate that I was able to return to my previous catering job when I returned from Africa. It gave me some stability and room to breathe and think about my next step.

It was May 1991.

I knew I had tough decisions ahead. There wasn't anything 'wrong' with the path I was on, but it no longer felt like the right path for me. What's more, I couldn't walk away from what I'd decided in Africa.

I wanted to find work that allowed me to do something that I loved.

But what?

I remember feeling scared about this desire to change my direction. After all, change meant an unknown future. In comparison, if I stayed where I was there was a degree of stability.

I felt as though I was standing on a cliff. Should I take a leap of faith and follow my heart, or should I continue within the safety of catering because it was what I knew?

I found the jump analogy far too daunting and so I transformed the image into crossroads. I realised it was simply about making a choice and a decision. With this understanding, it became far easier to take action.

I was ready for my next challenge... I wasn't sure what it would be but I was constantly thinking about and researching jobs, which allowed me to be creative.

John Wilkinson, my lovely boss at Aramark was very supportive and knew how I felt. I was fortunate that he offered me a job within the company to create the artwork and assets for the new customer service training package and organising the image library along with other small graphic design jobs. But I knew it wasn't quite what I was looking for.

I researched what other people had done to find what they were looking for. I read about Anita Roddick's Fairtrade cause and her travels to India. I know it sounds like a cliché to go to India to 'find yourself', but I felt this would be an incredible experience. I also knew it was an adventure I wanted to do by myself.

I bought a travel guide – the Lonely Planet Guide, together with a one-month return ticket to India, and hopped on a plane to Delhi. It was the 27th December 1991. I travelled mainly in the North West to Rajasthan. This included Jaipur, Jodhpur, Udaipur and over to Agra. I wasn't aiming to tick places off a 'visited list' but to immerse myself as much as possible in the culture. I spent a week learning how to do miniature Mughal style paintings. I also sketched, wrote and enjoyed the peace and solitude as well as the company of many friendly travellers and locals I met along the way.

It was a thoughtful and special time and I feel very fortunate to have been able to give myself this space when I needed it most.

I often think in life that it's important to be kind to ourselves. This doesn't always mean doing the easy stuff, but doing the things that are good for us. Taking time out for my solo trip to India was wonderful for my soul. I still start and end my day with three things I'm grateful for. I find it a good grounding activity and it replenishes my emotional bank with positive and nurturing thoughts.

When I returned to the UK, I felt assured that not only would I find my next creative endeavour, but I would also unlock the confidence I needed to step out of my comfort zone and do everything I could to find my fulfilling career.

I'd met Duncan a couple of weeks before my trip to India.

We both worked for a contract catering company and my sister Fran worked with Duncan. I was excited to see how this newfound friendship would develop on my return home.

I'm not exactly sure how it happened, but the work I wanted seemed to appear.

Inspiration hit...

I was back in London and committed to leave the contract catering company within four weeks when I decided to get a print that I loved framed – the picture is the Hay Barns by Van Gogh. It was a wake-up call. As I handed over my £70 to the picture framer it dawned on me that I could do that. Four bits of wood and a piece of glass for £70.

My decision was made...

I was going to be a picture framer so I left my job in catering management and waved goodbye to a secure salary and holiday pay. The company was very supportive and offered me a part-time role. This fixed, short-term contract gave me time to breathe and I used this job as a safety blanket whilst I created my next steps and made the change to 'full-time creativity'.

At the time, picture framing was perfect for me. It was hands-on, involved looking at lots of art, and I could make a living from it as there were people, like me, who would pay £70 to get a picture framed.

I applied to a number of picture framers for work and a lovely shop in Fulham gave me a job as their trainee. Yes it was a low wage, but I was doing something that made me smile every day.

What's slightly strange is when I was a catering manager I didn't know there were other jobs I could even apply for.

As Malcolm Gladwell says in his book **What the Dog Saw**,

> "To a worm in horseradish the world is horseradish."
>
> **Malcolm Gladwell, What the Dog Saw** (4)

It hadn't occurred to me until I really started to look for the opportunities that a creative career was a real possibility. But when I was committed, opportunities seemed to pop up.

You've probably experienced this yourself.

Say you're thinking about buying a red car. Before you know it, you'll start to spot red cars everywhere. The bizarre thing is they were always there, you just weren't tuned in to see them before.

One name for this phenomenon is "frequency illusion". Stanford linguistics professor Arnold Zwicky coined this phrase to describe the curious experience when a thing that's top of your mind seems to suddenly appear everywhere.

Despite what it looks like, it's not a coincidence that things crop up. We filter our world subconsciously. It's therefore important to be aware of the fact that our thoughts and ideas directly influence our lives.

At the same time I enrolled in Roehampton College and completed an Arts Management diploma and worked voluntarily in Arts and Business. This was a group that supported artists with business mentoring.

In 1995, Duncan and I moved to Marlborough where I found a new place to work in a very quirky framing workshop in Pewsey.

During my first few months in this job I was taught how to assemble frames by a 15-year-old lad who was just fabulous. He showed me how to cut wood, "as if you are slicing through butter." In Marlborough, the frames got bigger and more complex. We often worked on huge frames for a number of London galleries - making them look deliberately old.

It was a detailed, hands-on process.

First, we would build the frame and then gesso it (that's adding a thin layer of white clay). Next, we'd sand the frame before adding a layer of red clay. We'd sand again and finish with a gild of gold leaf before making the frame look aged. I recall that once we made a frame that was so big it wouldn't fit through the double doors of the studio!

I was in my element doing this work. I loved using my hands to make something from scratch. I loved all the textures and colours and I loved that we could transform ordinary materials into something quite beautiful.

Should I admit that my nickname was "Smasher"?

Unfortunately, this wasn't because I was 'smashing' at picture framing. Instead, it was a reference to my lack of glass assembly skills. This nickname stuck permanently after the unfortunate situation with the priceless antique the four seasons, large Chinese ceramics we were framing for the owner of a Chinese bank.

Spring, summer, and autumn went beautifully, but winter somehow slipped out of my hands and landed on its corner.

A deathly silence fell across the workshop as I announced the ceramic had cracked badly but was somehow still intact. The owner Phillip stormed over. He took the ceramic away and disappeared for the rest of the day to get it restored. He didn't speak to me for two weeks. I was told he must have liked me because when bad stuff happened, tins or brushes were thrown at you, or you were told to leave and never darken the workshop again.

But I did feel terrible. Letting someone down like that was just an awful feeling. Somehow, I lasted about a year there and I eventually progressed to creating the frames, but I was always known as 'Smasher'.

Framing was a far cry from the restrictions I'd felt in catering management and I remain very grateful for the tuition and patience of the people I worked with. We had a lot of fun and I loved working in a creative hands-on environment. This was the beginnings of a creative career that is still evolving to this day.

And now time for you

There is nothing more fulfilling than doing something you love. Often the thing you love draws you in and before you know it time flies. This is often called 'getting into the zone' or 'getting into the flow' and it describes a time when we're fully focussed and absorbed with the activity we're involved in.

The opposite feelings such as disappointment or discontentment can occur when we regularly do things that make us sad or compromise our personal values.

That's why it's so liberating to choose things that make you happy and capitalise on your skills and talents.

When trying to figure out what these things may be, it can be helpful to focus on what matters to you and what you can control.

Identifying the areas you can change and control often provides a greater clarity on what areas of your life you want to spend more time enjoying or developing.

This can of course feel a bit terrifying.

It can lead to tough decisions as well as letting go of certain habits, a job, a relationship, or beliefs. It's challenging because it's a step out of your 'known' comfort zone.

But these 'scary' steps are often the door to fulfilment, happiness, and an awakening of your real skills and talents.

When faced with a choice of staying put or trying something new, I often find it helpful to tap into my intuition. It usually guides me to the right answer because the insight it provides is made up of experiences, knowledge and feelings.

When I've trusted my head, heart and gut, things have generally turned out alright (or even pretty good) in the end.

Have a think about your own life.

When have you trusted your instinct and made a decision to take a different path? How did it work out? In comparison, are there times when you've not followed your instinct and have been left disappointed as a result?

By reflecting on these experiences, you can get clearer on the things that you choose. You can also learn how to show your children to tap into and trust their own inner wisdom as well.

Creativity meets business – completing the jigsaw

After working as a picture framer, I was certain my future was in creativity. I was keen to learn more and I was thrilled to complete my diploma in Arts Management at Roehampton College.

With this qualification under my belt, I set up my first business – Artworks.

Under the Artworks brand I created functional papier mâché art pieces including mirrors, clocks and tables. I sold these to various London shops as well as at my stall in Camden Market.

Friends will tell you I'd often be seen cycling home with boxes and bits of wood on the back of my bike – treasures I'd found that were ready to be transformed into something else with my imagination.

Recalling the cutlery from my John Lewis childhood, I'd find inspiration in the most unusual of places and was always on the lookout for colours, textures, and unique objects to inspire my thinking and create new, beautiful pieces.

I knew I was onto something with my work when Greenpeace commissioned me to create their tenth anniversary T-shirt. This commission gave me a huge sense of pride and achievement. It felt as though my passion, will, and desire to succeed were coming together – slowly!

In 1995, Duncan was looking to move on from catering management and was offered a job as Facilities Manager at Exeter University.

I continued to trade as Artworks and worked as a picture framer too. I wasn't sure where my creative energy would lead me, but I felt that my management skills and creative passion would spearhead into something. But I didn't know what.

What I did know was in order to develop my creative skills; I wanted to work on my ideas. With the massive support of Duncan, I decided to invest in further learning as I felt it would help me get to the next step.

Until this point I'd been largely self-taught. I wanted to study more formally so I enrolled onto an art foundation course at Exeter College.

It was absolutely fabulous.

I realised I'd felt like a square peg in a round hole for many years, but finally I'd discovered my space and I loved it.

What's more, this newfound confidence allowed me to get more adventurous with my creative thinking, problem-solving skills, and my creations.

I began experimenting with concrete and copper. I created paper clocks and glass lights. I created 'forms' by mixing plaster of Paris and filling the wok with this mixture – Duncan never quite knew what kitchen or household implement would be out of bounds and no longer available for normal usage.

My glass bowls were really popular. I created these by putting plaster of Paris in a wok to let it harden – this created the shape that I wanted. I then turned the mould upside down and put a circle of glass on the top. As the glass melted in the kiln, it took on the curved shape of the wok. I also added some ceramic colouring and popped it all into a super hot kiln for eight hours.

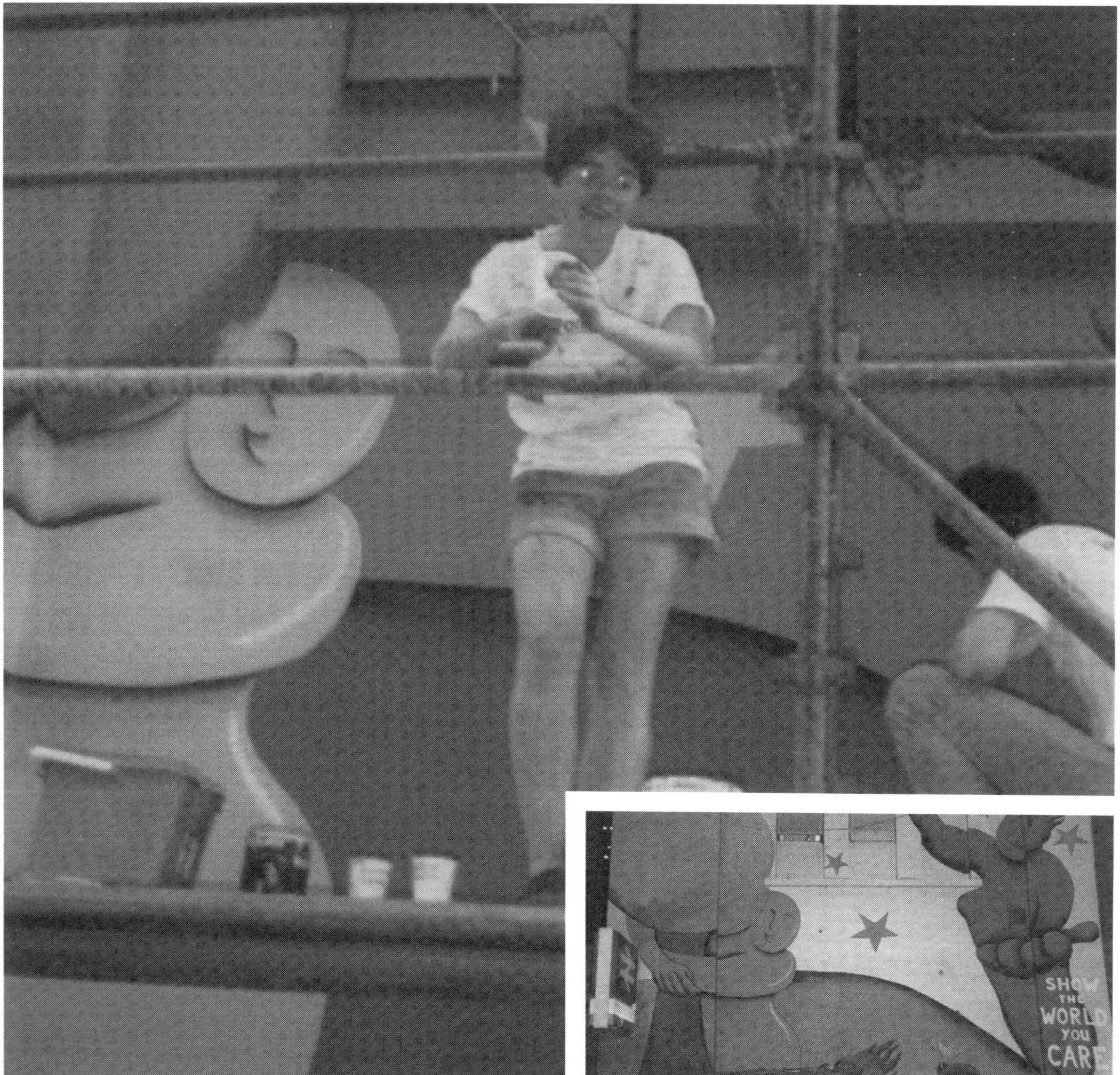

A 30ft tall mural friends and I painted at Charing Cross Station in London. The design was based on the T-shirt design used to raise funds for my Operation Raleigh expedition.

This would 'slump' or melt the glass to create rather unusual bowls.

My pieces were selling well and my bedroom studio had turned into a bit of a production line. But even though I was doing something that I loved, it surprised me that the success felt a little bit empty.

I was thrilled that people enjoyed and invested in my work. But something was missing... Yes I was being creative, but I really wanted to use that skill to help others and make a difference. It was the same instinct I'd felt when watching footage of the Ethiopian famine and it was just as strong now.

Tragically Duncan's mum died in 1996. Pat was a truly wonderful lady and we still miss her to this day. Duncan and I married in 1997. We had our evening do in my mum's beautiful garden and enjoyed a brilliant day with family and friends in one of the heaviest rain storms I can recall! (In 2017, we celebrated our first twenty years with lots of family and friends. I was thrilled to be able to get back into my wedding dress - which still had memorable splatters of mud across the back). We visited our wonderful family friends Molly and Wells in Maine and went sailing around the British Virgin Islands.

By now I'd finished my foundation degree, which freed up time to do some voluntary work alongside Artworks. After doing some research I approached a local group called Headway that helps people with head injuries. I loved it.

And word must have got around. I was soon invited to take up the role of head of art and design at a local Disabled Young Adult Centre (DYAC) and to provide their creative activities. It was a three-day a week contract and so it fitted with my studio work perfectly. It was the opportunity I'd been looking for – the chance to use my creative skills to help others.

I grabbed the chance and got stuck in.

Part of my new role was to set up a dark room and teach photography. When asked to set up a dark room, I was very tempted to jump up, turn off the light, and say ta-da!

Instead, I said I would need to do some research first, but I could definitely help. You see I didn't know the first thing about photography, but I knew I could learn a new skill.

All I needed was to find someone to teach me.

The centre manager was happy with that. I contacted a local photographer and paid him £25 an hour to help me get up to speed. I soon picked up enough skills to share my newfound knowledge with my students.

That's the thing in life... sometimes we don't have everything we need to make the most of a chance that comes our way. But if it feels right, you often have to grab it – and where there is a will, there is often a way to fill in the missing blanks.

I loved working at DYAC and I met and supported some phenomenal people.

During class, I would help my students create, explore, and develop their ideas. We'd often have exploratory sessions where I'd encourage the students to 'play' with materials and photography techniques to see what would happen.

This is the same approach we take with The Creation Station activities. Here's why...

When it comes to nurturing creativity, the end result is less important than the journey itself. By giving my students the freedom to experiment and express themselves, it enabled them to design their own creative adventure. Their activities were based on what interested them and what sparked their own imagination... Not the compromise that happens when someone else sets the boundaries, the rules, and the criteria.

The same goes for children. If you provide the opportunity for your child to explore ideas and discover a range of techniques and processes, they will develop a wide variety of skills from the activities you offer – including self-esteem and problem-solving as well as owning their learning.

There is of course a place for teaching a process or a method in order to help someone learn. This, dovetailed with the permission to experiment without doing it 'wrong', can really help to encourage people's own ideas and build confidence in themselves.

The results of the 'creative adventure' approach at DAYC were incredible...

Despite their physical challenges, when given the safe space and permission to explore, my students were empowered and had remarkable ideas.

There was one young man in particular who I am privileged to have worked with and will treasure our time together. His name was Barry.

Barry had an incredible imagination and a great sense of humour. Despite limited speech and movement, he embraced photography. To help, we set up a button on the headrest of his wheelchair so he could take pictures by pressing the button with his head. When we talked about subjects to photograph, Barry wasn't keen on going to the park; he wanted to go to the recycling centre.

As a result, Barry created a wonderful collection of photographs of bins. We put on an impressive art exhibition of the students' work. I was delighted my framing skills were put to good use and was able to mount and frame all the work. We then created a gallery and Barry's 'Bin' photos took pride of place at the council offices in Exeter for a number of years. Barry's sense of achievement was enormous and that gave the team and I a huge sense of satisfaction.

I knew I'd found myself.

I saw how a creative approach could transform people's lives – and it felt incredible to be a part of that journey.

And now time for you

Each and every one of us has immense potential. The problem is that many of us are limited by our beliefs and fear of failure. As such, we can feel too scared to even try.

But whether your glass is half full or half empty, it can still be topped up.

As parents, it's so tempting to protect our children from disappointment. But our own insecurities and concerns can actually limit what a child believes is possible for them.

Have a go at letting go...

Give your child opportunities to shine and sit back and watch. Let their journey unfold and resist the temptation to interfere or set expectations. What your children deliver may surprise you.

Here's a simple creative challenge to try – this activity can help your child make decisions and problem-solve whilst building their confidence.

Invite your child to take three things and then use them to create an object that can help make the world a better place.

1. Set a timer for 10-30 minutes depending on how long you feel they will sit for. You can always add on a bonus of fifteen minutes if they're still engrossed in the challenge.

2. Encourage your child to go through the recycling and choose their items. The rules are they can use three different objects such as boxes, plastic tubs and wool etc.

3. In addition, they are allowed things to attach the objects together such as tape, glue, string etc. Masking tape is an especially good fixer because you can paint or draw on it.

Younger children can get involved too. Share the journey with them and ask them to decide what three items they want to use. Talk about what would make their world a better place. It might be an ice cream maker, or a mummy tickling machine. Whatever your child invents just have some fun and let them decide.

Ask older children to decide how long they would like to spend on the activity. The more they are in control of the 'rules' the more involved and empowered they feel.

Adults can join in as well! Here are some examples from our Creation Station classes.

It's amazing what you can create from a shampoo bottle, some clay, matchsticks, a few felt pens, and coloured card.

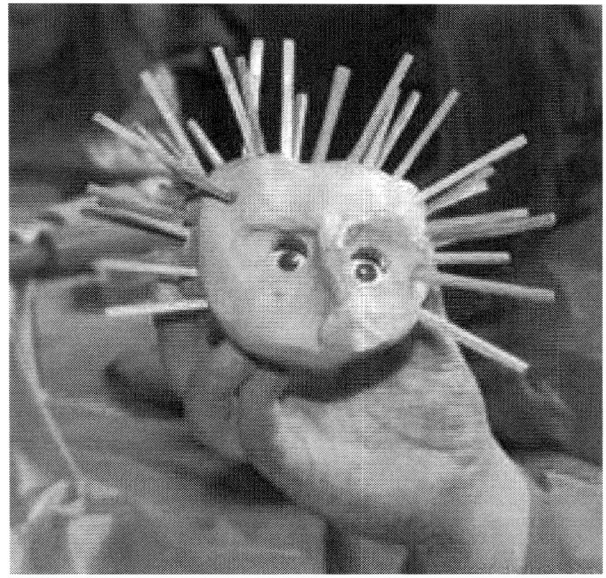

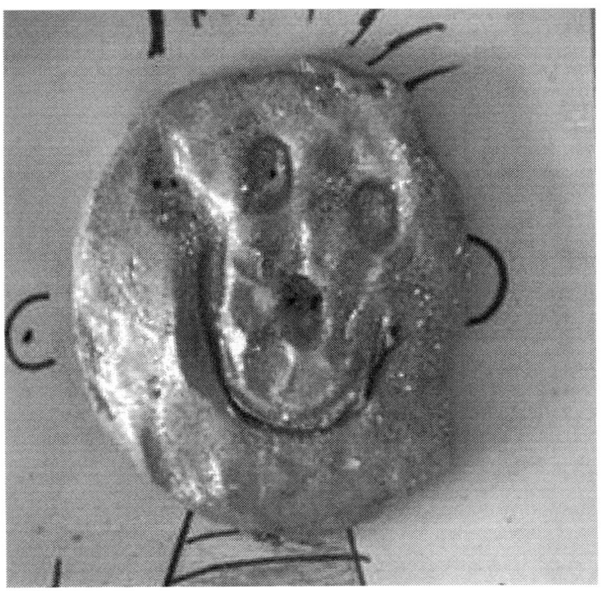

Getting the best job in the world

When you're a child, if you like mint choc chip ice-cream, you think everyone likes it.

It's only as we grow up we learn that other people not only like different things, but also think differently to us as well. This can lead to what psychologists call 'theory of mind'. This is the ability to imagine what other people may be thinking or feeling. Evidence from Wimmer & Perner 1983 (5) suggests that from around the age of six, children can start to understand that other people may have different thoughts to them.

Even as adults, it's not until we walk in someone else's shoes that we can truly understand what it feels like to be in their situation.

For me, and other people I've spoken with, becoming a parent provided a totally different perspective on my own parents and also life in general.

It felt like walking through a mirror and seeing everything with fresh eyes. And with three little boys I certainly could have benefited from a few extra sets of eyes plus an extra arm or two as well.

(When we run creative workshops, we have a tool kit, which always has emergency googly eyes!)

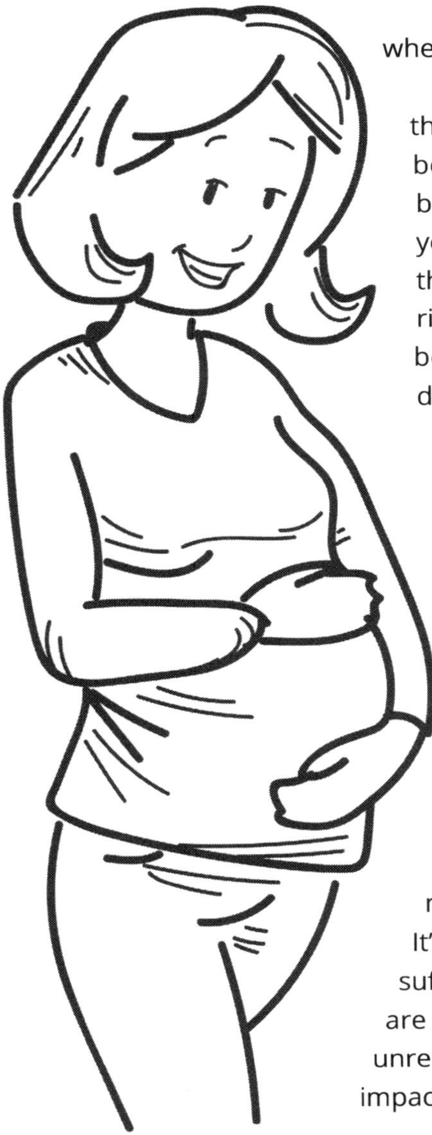

I became a mum at 1.20am on 1st December 1998 when we welcomed Sam into the world.

Sleepless nights, utter exhaustion, and more tears than you knew were possible. Sleep at 2.45am only to be woken again at 3.12am. Your heart in your throat because of constant worry and concern. The worry that you're not good enough, not knowing if you are doing the right thing, lots of conflicting advice. Not knowing the right answer because you've never heard the question before and wondering why everyone else seems to be doing a better job or coping better than you.

Sound familiar?

I think if it was widely known just how tough parenting really is, the world's population growth could grind to a halt.

It is incredibly tough, and you can feel very isolated and feel like you have lost yourself. This along with sleep deprivation can have a very negative effect.

It is reported that between 10% and 20% of women develop mental health problems during pregnancy or within a year of giving birth - this is called the 'perinatal' period. Around 50% of perinatal mental health problems are untreated or undetected. It's not only mums. It is reported that 10% of dads suffer from postnatal depression, and one in three dads are worried about their own health. This can often go unrecognised and untreated and can have a devastating impact on people, relationships and families.

A study commissioned by Welch's Grape Fruit Juice (6) and reported by Good Housekeeping revealed that if you add up the time the average working mum spends at her paid position and her duties at home, it totals 98 hours per week. When you work it out is the equivalent of two full-time jobs. That really doesn't leave much time left for all the other things including sleeping does it? Although the report didn't cover dads, I know it's the same for many dads too.

If you are able to find support to help you through these incredibly tough periods, parenting can be one of life's most rewarding and challenging of all journeys. You can feel like it's Christmas and your birthday all rolled into one. Your heart has a capacity for love you never knew existed. You take pride in each achievement your child makes and your whole body tingles with such emotion you think you're going to burst with joy.

Children change everything, as you'll know if you're also a parent or an aunt, uncle or family friend. And the changes can happen before they even enter the world.

For example, in May 1998, just three months into my pregnancy, I found myself with very limited mobility. It happened all of a sudden. Duncan was cleaning our windows and I was holding the ladder when suddenly I had to sit down immediately. I couldn't stand up and I couldn't walk.

Every movement I made was excruciating.

I was really frightened and I had no idea why...

It turned out I had a problem called Symphysis Pubis (SMP) – you may have heard of it.

SMP is quite severe and it meant I couldn't stand for more than a minute or so. It was like having sprained ankles, but around your hips. Anyway, I had to adapt, but fortunately I knew just the place to get a wheelchair – the good people at DYAC.

Fortunately, I was okay driving so I carried on working.

I used to drive into work, jump into a wheelchair, and carry on teaching and supporting the students with their wonderful creative activities.

However, it did get increasingly difficult, so as my pregnancy progressed I decided to leave DYAC, ditch the concrete mixing, and take up sewing instead so I could create things sitting down.

This step was important. I'd allowed myself to recognise my limitations and adapt my lifestyle accordingly.

The doctors said there was a high probability that I would be able to walk again in future, so I just needed to literally sit tight and wait.

I was understandably pretty devastated. Physically I was able to cope but emotionally it was really tough. I'd have a good cry about once a week and find ways to make the most of my situation rather than be crushed by it.

I turned my lack of mobility into an opportunity to have a change and I embraced the chance to explore a range of creative ideas by using a sewing machine. Being creative really did give me back my sanity. When I felt stuck, I pulled out my sewing machine and I could spend hours creating 3D images. It also helped give me some control over my circumstances and helped me find freedom and joy in my creative adventures. The 3D hand and machine stitched Christmas cards I made that year were true labours of love!

I feel very fortunate to have three great boys, Sam, Ollie and Josh. Sam was three and a half when I had Josh and the SMP showed up in all three of my pregnancies with progressive severity.

Things don't always go to plan, do they?

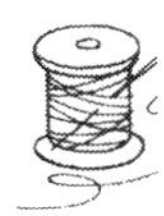

Whilst I loved being a mum, emotionally, it was tough being in a wheelchair with limited mobility for around two years in total. I'm forever grateful for the support from Duncan, my mum, my family and my friends for sticking by me and helping me out during those tricky times. Everyone was amazing.

I was also grateful for my ability to make the most of my situation and find enjoyment in a creative activity.

Whenever I felt stuck or frustrated, I'd get the boys involved in a fun creative activity and enjoy the simple fascination that children have in the world around them.

Looking back, this experience was yet another reminder of the power of creative activities and how it can help us to deal with challenging situations effectively.

I think Rudyard Kipling's poem 'If'. sums this up beautifully.

We used to have this on a tea towel over the kitchen table when I was growing up. I used to read it every morning, whilst I had my bowl of cornflakes.

Rudyard Kipling's If. (7)

If you can keep your head when all about you
Are losing theirs and blaming it on you,
If you can trust yourself when all men doubt you,
But make allowance for their doubting too;
If you can wait and not be tired by waiting,
Or being lied about, don't deal in lies,
Or being hated, don't give way to hating,
And yet don't look too good, nor talk too wise:

If you can dream - and not make dreams your master;
If you can think - and not make thoughts your aim;
If you can meet with Triumph and Disaster
And treat those two impostors just the same;
If you can bear to hear the truth you've spoken
Twisted by knaves to make a trap for fools,
Or watch the things you gave your life to, broken,
And stoop and build 'em up with worn-out tools:

If you can make one heap of all your winnings
And risk it on one turn of pitch-and-toss,
And lose, and start again at your beginnings
And never breathe a word about your loss;
If you can force your heart and nerve and sinew
To serve your turn long after they are gone,
And so hold on when there is nothing in you
Except the Will which says to them: 'Hold on!'

If you can talk with crowds and keep your virtue,
Or walk with Kings - nor lose the common touch,
If neither foes nor loving friends can hurt you,
If all men count with you, but none too much;
If you can fill the unforgiving minute
With sixty seconds' worth of distance run,
Yours is the Earth and everything that's in it,
And - which is more - you'll be a Man, my son!

And now time for you

It's important to accept that things don't always go to plan and that some things are out of our control. Parenthood in particular thrusts a huge amount of change into our lives. The best coping mechanism I know of is to adapt.

As humans, we're far more creative and resilient than we think. Using our imagination, we have the power to create, problem-solve, and adapt. We can work around obstacles and challenges – sometimes even creating a better outcome.

How do you respond to change and challenges? Are you adaptable, or do you feel stuck when life doesn't work out as planned?

Reflect back upon your life at key events where you've felt out of control. How did you handle them? What would you do differently if you had your time over? What will you do next time your status quo shifts?

Children learn from the way you react and behave. Make some notes in the space below, about what attitudes to change you'd like to explore with them.

Am I doing it right?

How do you know if you're doing the best for your child? What should you teach them? What values should you instil in them? How much screen time is appropriate? How much freedom should they have?

In a world where we're increasingly connected and where information is at our fingertips, childhood is very different from what we experienced as kids. And one common concern raised by parents is how we can equip our children to cope with this fast-paced world.

The website parenting.com (8) surveyed 1,000 mums and dads to find some answers to the question of new family values.

Religion scored the highest, the reason given is because it can provide a strong foundation.

Family time together was also cited as being a really important factor. What's more, the same survey also came up with the 'Fab Five' – the most desirable character traits for kids. Perhaps these traits reflect some of your own values.

- Honesty
- Strong self-esteem
- Kindness
- Good manners
- Strong work ethic

It's tough when you become a parent, as we know children don't come with an instruction manual. And if you have more than one, they are remarkably different and may need a different approach to your other children. So how do you know what to do for the best so that you can raise kids who are happy, healthy, and able?

Like most parents, I was very conscious about giving Sam, Ollie and Josh the best possible start. I wanted to be able to feel that I was a good mother. I don't know about you, but at times I found it so confusing! Everyone has an opinion on parenting and there's so much conflicting advice. From how to help your child sleep, to the foods they should eat, to the clothes they should wear and the activities they should do – who's right?

My two youngest children would wake every two hours. Unfortunately, they weren't the same two hours so going to bed just felt like a night shift. It was exhausting. I tried lots of things that other people swore by and eventually came to the conclusion that there is no 'one size fits all' solution.

Sure there are the 'fundamentals' which apply to children of any age such as eye contact, listening, smiling, encouraging, and guiding. And I bet you're doing an amazing job at these already.

As Sue Atkins the renowned television presenter and parenting expert says:

> "There is no such thing as a perfect parent so just be a real one."
>
> ***Sue Atkins Inspiring Sunday Saying*** (9)

In Ollie's case, I tried everything to help him settle. I eventually discovered fennel seeds. I'd put a teaspoon of the seeds into a jug of boiling water. When the water cooled, I gave him a teaspoon. It really helped settle his tummy. But the real problem turned out to be milk. When Ollie switched to goat's milk his sleep improved almost overnight.

The lesson here is that every child is unique.

What works for one parent may not work for you, and similarly what works for one child may not work for another – and that's OK. Instead, I learnt that you have to trust your instincts and do what you feel is right for you, your child, and your family.

This insight reduced my anxiety and boosted my confidence significantly. It just made sense. After all, have you ever met two people who are exactly the same?

No, me neither.

I've come close… my husband has an identical twin and while they may look alike, their personalities are different.

And every parent and child is different too…

We've all had a different journey to parenthood. I've talked about this already, but the paths we've chosen, the places we've been, the people we've met, and the things we've done have all shaped our dreams, behaviours, fears, and beliefs. And when I was trying to figure out what to do for my children I realised that my own experiences and values held the key to knowing what was right for my boys.

My mum had done the same. She wanted us to have the ability to cope with whatever came our way – an instinct that I still have in bounds. It's why she encouraged us out of our comfort zones and supported us to do things that were challenging. It's why she encouraged me to go to boarding school and why she supported my choice to go to the Kibbutz. Coping – or grit – is an instinct I've developed that serves me well.

> "The confidence your child has in their abilities to solve a problem, make a difference, or change their circumstances. Grit is sticking to your goals and not letting obstacles get in your way".
>
> ***Angela Duckworth, Grit***
> (10)

When I was deciding what I wanted to teach my boys, the first place I looked was my own life.

I recognised the richness I got from travelling and exploring the world – I'd like that for my kids too. And because of the wealth that art and creativity has brought into my life, I'm passionate about weaving creative thinking and problem-solving into my children's routine as well.

I've also been blessed with a brilliant and supportive partner, Duncan. And of course Duncan's life influences our children's too. Duncan always talks about the 'wonder within'. This has helped our boys to respect, value, and appreciate their world. It's helped them to blossom into the amazing, spirited boys that they are.

I know I've been fortunate to have enjoyed a wide range of

experiences with my life so far. When many of my peers were staying at home, I was off to Africa, Israel, India and travelling across America. I was taking risks and living life – because that's what I felt compelled to do.

And I want to nurture this in my children too – because I've seen and experienced first-hand, the amazing things that can happen when you just go for it.

But I realise to do this, you need confidence, resilience, and self-belief – among other skills and characteristics.

But how could I teach and instil these empowering values in my children?

Between us, Duncan and I had a sense of the values we hoped our boys would share and demonstrate. We spent a bit of time chatting this through.

We now have our Family Guide. We have it up on the boiler cupboard as a constant reminder of what is important to each other and our family.

This is a simple but effective thing to do no matter what age the children are. Of course, our current guide is a little different to that very first one. Whilst our core values have remained the same, Duncan and I have grown – as have the boys.

That's why we periodically review our guide and get the boys' input to ensure our guide speaks to how our family is right now.

Family Guide

And now time for you

What's your deepest wish for your child beyond being happy? Do you want your child to share your religious beliefs, value honesty, be tolerant, and respect others – or perhaps a mixture of these?

A powerful way to nurture behaviours and character traits that you value in your children is with your own Team or Family guide. Once completed, this can provide a reminder as to what's important to you, your partner and your family.

Here are some suggestions to help you get started:

Step 1: Get clear about your values.
Review the list of life values below.

- First, tick the ten values which are most important to you
- Next rank these in order of importance from 1–10
- Finally, choose the two which you value the most and the two which you value the least

- ☐ Achievement
- ☐ Assertiveness
- ☐ Beauty
- ☐ Caring
- ☐ Challenging work
- ☐ Cleanliness
- ☐ Compassion
- ☐ Confidence
- ☐ Consideration
- ☐ Courage – physical and of convictions
- ☐ Courtesy
- ☐ Creativity
- ☐ Determination
- ☐ Enthusiasm
- ☐ Excellence
- ☐ Faith in oneself
- ☐ Faith in God
- ☐ Faithfulness
- ☐ Flexibility
- ☐ Forgiveness
- ☐ Friendship
- ☐ Generosity
- ☐ Gentleness

- [ ] Health
- [ ] Helpfulness
- [ ] Honesty
- [ ] Honour
- [ ] Humility
- [ ] Idealism
- [ ] Independence
- [ ] Integrity
- [ ] Joyfulness
- [ ] Justice
- [ ] Kindness/empathy
- [ ] Knowledge
- [ ] Love
- [ ] Loyalty
- [ ] Mercy
- [ ] Moderation
- [ ] Modesty
- [ ] Morality
- [ ] Obedience
- [ ] Orderliness
- [ ] Patience
- [ ] Peacefulness
- [ ] Personal growth
- [ ] Pleasure
- [ ] Power
- [ ] Purposefulness
- [ ] Recognition
- [ ] Reliability
- [ ] Religion
- [ ] Respect for self and others
- [ ] Responsibility
- [ ] Reverence
- [ ] Security
- [ ] Self-discipline
- [ ] Self-esteem
- [ ] Service
- [ ] Steadfastness
- [ ] Tact
- [ ] Thankfulness/gratitude
- [ ] Tolerance
- [ ] Trust
- [ ] Trustworthiness
- [ ] Truthfulness
- [ ] Wealth
- [ ] Wisdom

Step 2: Turn the values into actions.
Once you've identified your values, the next step is to turn these into phrases that you want to nurture and promote in your family 'team'. Here are a few thoughts to get you started.

- If love was important to you, you might say something like, 'We will love each other unconditionally.'
- If you chose integrity, you may write, 'We will be honest and truthful with each other.'
- If you chose gratitude, you may say, 'We pick something each day, which we are grateful for.'

Step 3: Pin it up
Finally, create something beautiful with your Team or Family Guide. Involve your children and you can create something visual and personal. Once created place your guide somewhere that it can be constantly seen. It will serve you well.

Setting goals and the birth of a creative business

When Duncan and I reflected on our values we realised some things had to change.

As a mum, my perspective had altered. Whilst I was lucky to have an extremely rewarding and flexible business – running Artworks and running creative workshops at DYAC, this work no longer gave me what I needed as a mum.

Duncan and I talked at length about what we wanted for our boys, our family, and ourselves – and we wrote down some personal goals:

My top priority was to be there for my children. I wanted to pick them up from school, be there to wipe their tears, to cuddle them often and share their happiness. I wanted to be free to play their games, read their books, and cherish watching them grow.

That said I also wanted to get out of the house and earn my own good income too. I loved being self-employed. It gave me a huge sense of purpose and satisfaction – especially when I was able to help others. Being a mum was my priority, but I instinctively knew that I needed to nurture my entrepreneurial spirit too. I knew my boys wouldn't be small for ever and I didn't want to lose myself in nappies and baby talk.

I wanted to continue to grow, explore my potential, and contribute to the family pot.

After running Artworks I'd got a taste of what it was like to create something bigger than myself. I wanted to build a business that had scope to grow as my kids got older.

My business had to make a difference to others too. Just like Anita Roddick, I wanted to build a business based on my values of contribution, creativity, and inspiration.

And it had to be fun! Ultimately, we all work hard, whether it's in a job or in our own business. I knew I'd be more motivated if I enjoyed what I did.

Once I'd written down and thought about what I wanted to create, my thinking became more focused.

Given my journey so far, I knew I wanted to use my creative skills and work with arts and crafts – it was where I was at my best. But it couldn't be in the same way as Artworks or DYAC because that model didn't include my children.

Despite being open to the possibility of a new business idea, I didn't have a clue about the detail. You may have had a similar experience. You've got a vague notion of what you want to do – such as starting a business that works around your children – but you're unclear about the specifics.

I found that putting my intention 'out there' was a start. I soon began to notice 'clues' that would previously have gone unnoticed. I had conversations that gave me clarity and I stumbled into experiences that helped me focus.

Often the answer pops up in the most unexpected places.

With not being very mobile because of my hip problems, it was quite hard meeting other mums. Like many others, I was going along to groups for my children but also so that I could meet and chat with other parents. But some of the groups I went to were very cliquey. It was hard to have a conversation with anyone. I often found myself feeling worse after attending some of these groups than before I went. I think this was a big factor for wanting to develop a relaxed, welcoming and shared creative activity group. I wanted to go somewhere where there was no right or wrong. It didn't matter if your child didn't sit down 'nicely' like everyone else's child. You can feel so judged – and my three would never all sit down at the same time.

I think some of the loneliness and frustration really helped spur me on to develop The Creation Station.

The idea was born out of a conversation with a good friend of mine, a great lady called Jan. Back in 2002, we got chatting about the importance of creative activities for children and identified the huge gap in the provision for children and parents to be creative, learn and develop together through fun, hands-on experiences.

"Wouldn't it be great to go somewhere like that?" we said...

It was a light-bulb moment.

I indeed had been frustrated that there weren't any 'good' creative groups where I could go with my kids. There wasn't a place to meet like-minded parents where the focus was helping children to blossom and develop their own skills, enabling them to achieve their own potential. I didn't know of any activity that nurtured each child, sparked their creativity and celebrated their journey. It could also enable parents and carers to easily chat whilst doing things with their children. This approach could hopefully provide a welcome space for other people who may be feeling like I did.

> "Others have seen what is and asked why. I have seen what could be and asked why not."
>
> ***Pablo Picasso***
> (11)

I realised I could set up experiences – just like the ones I wanted:

- I could use my creative and business experience
- The work was flexible so I could fit it around my children – I could take them with me!
- I could start small and grow at a rate and pace that suited my family
- I could support adults with a way of connecting and making friends with others.

It was definitely worth giving it a go.

And so The Creation Station was built around what I wanted for my children and with values that I shared with thousands of other mums and dads, grandparents and carers.

I recognised that through The Creation Station classes, I could do more to give my children the best possible start in life. It's always stuck with me that a child's brain changes from the size of a tangerine to a grapefruit in their first few early years.

In the first year of life, when critical emotional components of the brain are being formed, a secure and predictable environment is most important, including lots of touching and having needs met promptly.

Also key to brain development in the first three years is being talked to, being played with, and having a varied, stimulating environment – balanced by opportunities to rest, which is when the brain reorganises itself.

These very simple but vital things set the stage for all later learning.

Surprisingly, the brain of a two-year-old has trillions of connections – double the number that an adult has. The brain grows connections in response to all kinds of input in order to be adaptable and survive. Over time, certain connections are used again and again while others fall by the wayside.

This may be one of the reason why children are like sponges. They soak up early experiences and learn at a rapid pace.

I wanted to be proactive and help my boys develop their confidence, learn about problem-solving, and understand more about their world and maintain and strengthen as many of these connections as was right for each of them.

And I knew positive arts and crafts activities could be the vehicle to help achieve this.

My time at DYAC had shown me what's possible when people are allowed to discover in a safe and fun environment. And I was excited about the opportunity to create a community where other people could gather, be creative, have fun and adult conversations and make new friends too.

My classes were an instant hit. To be honest, I never knew who was more excited when we did Creation Station activities – the kids or the adults!

It's a phrase we hear time after time from parents who come to our weekly classes; they love the value their child gets from the session, but they also love sharing the fun with other parents.

> "I don't know who loves our Creation Station classes more, me or Max. It's a journey of discovery for him and a return to childhood for me."
>
> ***Max's mummy. Attended one of my Little Explorer classes in 2008***

When building the business, I decided to think big right from the start...

I vividly remember standing at the island in my kitchen and thinking... "This business model could work really well for other people too." Recalling the words of my mum that I could do anything, I decided to create a model so that other people who shared my values could make a difference with their own Creation Station.

It was 2002. Josh was a month old, Ollie was 22 months, and Sam was 3 ½ years old and I'd just set a goal to create twenty franchises.

I was very fortunate. Duncan was hugely supportive and because he was the main breadwinner, I had the freedom and time to develop and test my programmes with help from my kids to ensure I got the activities and programmes just right.

With franchising in mind, I wanted to iron out as many of the hurdles as possible that can happen when you start up a business. I wanted to make delivery of our creative sessions so easy that if your kids had starved you of sleep you could almost deliver the session plan on autopilot.

Over the next five years, I ran my creative classes and learnt what I needed in terms of education, systems, support, purchasing, marketing, and cash flow.

It was great fun developing our programmes. You may be familiar with the phrase emotional intelligence. This is defined as the capacity to be aware of, control, and express our emotions while handling our relationships with good judgement and empathy.

I feel there is a place for Creative Intelligence too. There isn't a dictionary definition of this yet. I know it will be recognised and valued with increasing importance over the next few years. Here are some definitions of what Creative Intelligence is:

> "The ability to go beyond the existing to create novel and interesting ideas."
>
> ***Møller, 2005***
> (12)

My own definition is:

> "Harnessing the power to think, create, connect, and inspire."
>
> ***Sarah Cressall, 2017***

From what I have seen, read and experienced I agree that a creative approach does develop creative intelligence, because it helps us to think, make connections, create, and be inspired. I was keen to produce a curriculum that would enable children to develop the wide range of skills associated with these key life skills.

As well as learning from the children and adults who we were privileged to spend time with, we were inspired by research from a wide range of influences including: The Theory of Multiple Intelligence developed by Dr Howard Gardner (13), Steiner Waldorf, Maria Montessori, Edward de Bono's 'Creative Thinking' (14) and Emilio Reggio's '100 Languages of Children' (15).

I also spent time with child education experts and thankfully, some of my very clever friends were experts too including Elaine, Kerry, and Nicky. I worked with the British Franchise Association and a specialist franchise consultant. I focused on making the one percent improvement needed to the structure and blueprint model to make The Creation Station a viable and successful franchise opportunity.

At the same time, I enjoyed the flexibility I wanted for Sam, Ollie, Josh, and Duncan.

It was hard going to get everything developed from scratch and to be a mum too.

If the franchise had already been established I would have invested in it, as so many things are already set up for you. But it wasn't and I had a lot of work to do develop the business.

Juggling these things did take its toll.

When the boys were little, a friend came around who was very glamorous, and said to

me – I've never seen you dress nicely before. I'm sure she meant it as a compliment – but it made me realise that I just didn't have any energy to think about me. The next day, I decided to go and treat myself to some new clothes, so I popped out to Tesco's, as I knew they did clothes. It didn't occur to me that there were other perhaps more glamorous places to go. I accidentally used my lip liner as eyeliner. If I didn't look tired before I had done a fabulous job at looking well and truly bleary eyed.

The level of tiredness was certainly overwhelming, I recall enjoying going to the dentist as I could lie down, and not have do anything. I would often hear the words "If you can just try to stay awake that would be helpful Mrs Cressall."

With three under three and half it was exhausting. And if you have kids, I'm sure you will be able to relate to this. I used to go to the hairdressers with my kids - I would lay out a little picnic blanket and they would have a tea party on the floor whilst I got my hair cut. One day I was at the hairdressers and I noticed a huge stain on my top. I said to Jeff (my hairdresser for over twenty years) "Sorry – that's the problem when you have kids." Jeff said "What you do mean Sarah - that was you a minute ago – you've just managed to spill your coffee all over yourself."

It's easy to end up being at the bottom of the pile. However I look back on those years and love that fact I did have lots of time with my kids. Plus as I continued to get great feedback from my customers, I instinctively knew I was onto something and that The Creation Station would make a positive contribution.

And now time for you

What do you want for you and your child?

Take five minutes and write here what you want for your child. As their mummy, daddy, grandparent, or aunty, what do you want for their life?

Then repeat this exercise, but this time think about what you want for you.

Discovering my first franchise owner

Before I knew it, five years had flown by and Josh, my youngest, had started school. It was September 2007. It's the end of an era when your little one goes to school. For me it meant I had some more time to spend on my business. After receiving such lovely feedback from the families who attended my sessions, I was keen to create opportunities for children elsewhere in the country to get creative. I knew there was limited scope for me to expand without help and realised it was time to award my very first franchise.

Personally, this was a hugely proud moment. It was so satisfying to know that the time and hard work I'd invested into the franchise blueprint had been worthwhile.

There was a lot of interest in the franchise opportunity. With so many people showing interest, I took my time to choose the right person. Whilst I'd always imagined Creation Station franchises across the country, this wasn't about building a big business quickly. Instead I knew I needed the right advocates to help me – people who are proactive, fun and friendly with a good fit to our company's values.

have fun
nurture creativity
give care inspire imagination
ensure quality
engage learning

Like me, our franchise owners typically want the freedom to run their own business and the flexibility to work around their children or other commitments. They also have a desire to make a difference, nurture children's and adults' creativity, and help parents and carers unlock their child's potential.

The starting point for a new Creation Station franchise owner is to request an information pack, have a chat with us and then, if we both feel it could be the right fit, you are invited to attend one of the free monthly 'Discovery Events' we run. I love running these events. They always have a great energy and I've met many amazing people over the years.

To give you a flavour of what happens, I've shared a popular activity on the next 'And now time for you' idea. I think you'll find it thought-provoking.

I'm a big advocate of goal setting and we work with our franchise owners to help them with their vision for their future too.

Decisions are the tools which create our lives – and the more aware we are of what we want to have in the future, the more likely we are to take the steps needed to make those dreams and goals a reality.

Planning your life is important work. We often plan our holidays in more detail than we do our lives. With that in mind, this exercise is most definitely worth a few minutes of your time.

What's more, you may find this activity can help you to inspire your children too.

As you know, when you feel happy and fulfilled you feel better about your life, and yourself. And if you know what you want to create, and you've written it down, you can take proactive steps to make your goals a reality.

Taking positive action to achieve your goals is a powerful message to teach your children. It demonstrates how they too can be in control of their life and their destiny. As my mum said, if you want something enough, anything is possible.

And now time for you

It doesn't matter what your goal is, from meeting a friend to going shopping once a month to planning a once-in-a-lifetime holiday, it's helpful to strive for something so you have a forward focus and something to aim for.

1. Draw a line on a piece of paper

2. Write today's date to the left and the date five years from now on the right

3. Use the space in the middle to write down all the things you'd like to achieve or have in your life in the next five years
4. If you get stuck, think back five years – it doesn't seem that long ago, does it? Recall anything you're unhappy about, or things you love doing and would like more of in your life. Use that as a starting point to plan your next five years

Then create your five-year timeline and invite your children to get involved by asking them to talk about the things they'd like to have in their future.

Creative sparks

As word of The Creation Station spread, we received an increasing number of requests for more activities. I was open to new opportunities and ideas to expand our services – but only if there was an alignment with our core values.

I'd started out with Little Explorer classes – supporting preschool children aged 15 months to five years. This age group made sense because it fitted perfectly with my desire to do activities with my children before they went to school. But after a request from a children's centre in Leeds to run sensory development classes for younger children, Baby Discover classes were born.

We were asked to provide birthday parties. To help celebrate the most important day in not just a child's life, but their whole extended family, is a huge responsibility and privilege. We wanted to create something where all ages and girls and boys could have fun and get creative. Also, we wanted to provide a party entertainment package that was super easy for the parents. We developed our Arty Parties which include a great range of fun activities where each child creates at least two unique masterpieces, and these go into their personalised party bags. With party bags and invites included, these have been in huge demand since we launched them back in 2008.

Soon after, parents began to tell us that their older, school-aged children felt they were missing out. In response, we set up Family Fun sessions. Regardless of age or ability, our arts and crafts approach works really well if there's a mix of ages and so everyone can get creative together.

Next, schools, educational organisations, and nurseries began to get in touch and ask us to run creative after-school clubs for them. In response, we carefully developed a programme for older children and then piloted it and tweaked it in different parts of the country for over two years. When everything was good to go, we launched Create Club, which now runs in hundreds of schools right across the country.

We also have Saturday clubs and we work in partnership with different holiday camps to provide activities for them.

What we found was lots of the adults we met would say, can you do this for us grown-ups? So now we run Creative Crafters – adult crafts down the pub with Prosecco, or crafts afternoons in garden centres with tea and cake. They both go down really well and are great fun.

We now also provide Tiny Treasure creative keepsakes for new mums or dads and their new-borns, and we now provide this in nurseries.

New developments include the provision of Care and Creativity workshops with the elderly and bringing in our Little Explorers classes to provide intergenerational creative fun. It's such a wonderful experience; it's hard to put it into words.

It goes to show how a simple idea can quickly gain momentum and blossom into something far greater than you ever imagined. When I started my very first class all those years ago, I had no idea that my business would evolve so much.

I never anticipated getting into Event Entertainment – but this service naturally evolved as The Creation Station grew.

It all started with a big stand at the National Franchise Exhibition when we promoted The Creation Station opportunities. Our stand was bright, colourful and eye-catching. We caused a huge buzz and made an impact with people making models. We had a little competition to see what people could create in two minutes. It was such fun! Suddenly I realised...

"Wow, all ages love getting creative at events!"

At the time, I didn't realise what a game-changer this was going to be for us. Now we support event organisers with fun, hands-on activities, kidszones and crafts zones. We provide activities in shopping centres, town centres, parks, cinemas, cafes, galleries, garden centres and festivals to mention a few. We were the runner-up in the Festival Supplier awards and now events are a key element of our business.

The highlight was securing the contract for the 2012 Olympics in Hyde Park where we provided two weeks of fun creative experiences. As you can imagine the atmosphere was electric and it's an experience I will remember for the rest of my life. This is something that would never have happened unless we'd believed in our capabilities, opened ourselves to opportunities, and listened to our customers.

Partnerships and unexpected opportunities have been one of the most exciting developments at The Creation Station in recent years. For example, we've been privileged to work with a wide range of companies including Lego, Duplo, Sony, Bugaboo, Aardman, Hasbro, Marks and Spencer, Sainsbury's, Tesco, national chains of nurseries, garden centres, shopping centres and many great PR agencies. The journey has been unbelievable. We've been privileged to work with some amazing people and have enjoyed opportunities and experiences I would never have anticipated.

But it's not been all work, work, work.

Just as I wanted, my children have been involved since the beginning – first as participants and now as occasional helpers and advisors. Having tested and done many of the activities themselves they are brilliant at working with and supporting other children. I'm filled with immense pride to see them sharing their creative ideas and drawing upon the experiences they've had during their own Creation Station journey. I'm sure their lives are all the richer for the creative fun we've had on this brilliant adventure.

And of course, it's not just my children who have benefitted. I have calculated that since 2002, The Creation Station has reached and supported over 950,000 children, families and adults. And that's another goal achieved. I'm very proud that The Creation Station makes it possible for a two-year-old, a four-year-old, a nine-year-old, and their mum or granddad to sit and enjoy a range of creative activities together.

The Creation Station enables quality, fun, shared family experiences. At its heart, we're focused on putting creativity back into childhood.

We focus on the creative journey – not the final outcome. We don't make hats one session and then photo frames another. Instead, we explore ideas, provide inspiration and materials and encourage children to go on their own creative journey to explore, discover and develop in a way that sparks their own imagination.

And the results are amazing. I'm always impressed by the conversations, giggles and endless flow of ideas and smiles that children and parents have when their senses and imaginations are stimulated.

But don't just take my word for it! We receive reviews and emails overflowing with positive feedback almost everyday – praise that highlights our proactivity and the quality and enjoyment of our classes.

TRUSTPILOT

I'm proud that we're rated as a 5-Star activity provider on Trustpilot, with over two thousand reviews. I'm really grateful to our franchise owners for the passion, energy, and care they put into the creative experiences they deliver.

I'm constantly motivated to do more and improve. For me it's a privilege to meet and work with such amazing families. What's more I'm blown away by the calibre of our franchise owners. They 'get' what we are striving to do and know what we do matters.

You could say I've achieved my Anita Roddick inspired goal of creating a business that makes a difference – a goal I've had since I was a teenager.

But there's still more to do...

Everyone has heard of Crayola. It's an amazing brand with brilliant products.

Well, my mission is to make The Creation Station the household name for creative experiences, so that accessing positive creative activities is easier for everyone, whatever your age, ability or circumstances.

And we're getting there...

Today, The Creation Station is the only company in the UK that can provide creative experiences in any part of the country with local, caring franchise owners who are qualified first aiders, DBS checked, safeguarding trained, and health and safety trained.

I do believe a creative outlook can have so many positive outcomes.

And now time for you

When I look back, The Creation Station evolved and grew in the way it has because I was open to explore opportunities and suggestions as they were presented to me. If you had told me when I first started that we'd be involved in the London 2012 games I would have laughed! It just shows what's possible when you believe that anything is possible and you're willing to explore and experiment with new ideas that are perhaps out of your comfort zone.

As adults we can sometimes get caught with habits – only doing the things that we know. But new experiences can invigorate us. They also change our perception of what's possible by broadening our thinking and our knowledge about ourselves and the world around us.

What new things could you explore by yourself and with your family? Remember, when we discover with our children, it helps them to learn how to enjoy the unknown too.

Did you know…

The Creation Station logo was developed from one day waiting in the hairdressers with my three boys.

Sam, Ollie, Josh and I were creating shapes with our hands. If you look closely you can see that our famous 'splat' is actually two hands.

It's those special moments when we connect where the magic really happens.

This is one of the original designs, alongside our most recent brand logo.

Learning from setbacks

As The Creation Station grew so did the challenges. I didn't always get it right – but I know that setbacks, uncomfortable situations, and challenges are inevitable when you step out of your comfort zone and try new things.

For example, there was the time I received an invite to go to an Academy of Chief Executives meeting.

I have to be honest it didn't jump out as the sort of thing that really appealed to me, but I decided it would be good for me to go along. I thought spending time with Chief Executives and being in a room with a lot of men in suits would help me build up my confidence.

As it turned out, the meetings run by a lovely gentleman called William Waddington were really good and very informative. All the people I met were interesting, delightful, and good company. One month we decided to attend the next meeting in fancy dress, just for fun. I was always a few minutes late to the meetings as I was still walking my kids to school in the morning, so as I ran into the hotel in Exeter and spotted a gentleman in a checked shirt I smiled and thought, 'Ah, he must have come as a cowboy.'

But as I got closer to the group I noticed that everyone was wearing their usual attire. There was not a single fancy dress costume to be seen. I seriously wanted the ground to swallow me up! In that moment I realised I could either turn around and walk away or face up to it. I held my head high and walked in... with my knee-length boots and an all-in-one Mrs Incredible outfit.

There was a lot of laughing – mainly from them rather than from me – although I took it in good spirits. Then someone said, "You didn't get the email, Sarah?" I simply said, "What do you mean? This is my usual Tuesday outfit!"

In other words, when things don't work out the way you'd like or you expected, you still get to choose your response. I decided to push the embarrassment to one side and get stuck into the event. As it was about presentation skills including the chance to stand up and present, there was no hiding.

We worked with a wonderful guest speaker, Celia Delaney. Celia had been a great help to me previously with developing my presentation skills, so it was good to have her in the room. And after my experience on that day, I always have a positive to lean on whenever I'm feeling the pressure of standing up and delivering. At least I'm not wearing a rather tight Mrs Incredible outfit!

Another example was the very first time I was asked to do a birthday party back in 2007. I hadn't thought about offering a party service until this point, but as someone had asked, I thought I'd give it a go.

The parent wanted a choo-choo train theme so I came up with a great idea or so I thought! In reality it was quite complicated to make.

Unfortunately for me, the size of the party grew beyond the 15 children we'd agreed, but I hadn't been informed. On the big day I was confronted with 27 four-year-olds running riot in the small function room at the pub the parent had hired.

Deep breaths were required. That party may have been the longest hour of my life.

Somehow all the children managed to create their printed paintings with their own train picture frame with movable wheels. The lady was very happy, but did tell me that she thought I'd have more help. But I'd allowed her to negotiate my price right down so I couldn't afford any assistance. What's more, I hadn't thought to confirm final numbers.

I learnt quite a lot from this and developed the process to manage expectations and ensure we deliver a fabulously engaging and fun party for all ages.

We've now been privileged to provide our Arty Party entertainment for over 75,000 children's special birthday celebrations. We provide the invites, a selection of fun creative activities to suit all ages and budgets. Plus, parents love the fact that the party bags are all done for them and filled with each child's unique artworks.

You learn so much when things go wrong.

> "Keep your integrity in all you do. When things get tough it's an anchor to ensure you behave in a way that you are proud of."
>
> ***Sarah Cressall 2017***

Whilst 'failing' is not my preferred choice, it's inevitable that not everything will go as expected – especially when you're exploring things you've never tried before. You have a choice – to stay safe and turn an opportunity down. Or step up and give it a go to see what happens.

Guess which I prefer?

I don't mind failing. Feeling 'OK' if things do not go to plan has been fundamental to growing my business. I'd rather start with something, which I accept will not be the polished article, than procrastinate and never start at all. That way I can learn from my experiences and create an even better product as a result.

There is a great acronym for Fail:

FAIL

First Attempt In Learning

We are not likely to get everything right first time, but if we are too frightened of failing we will never learn or get better or eventually master the activity we were trying so hard to be good at.

It's the reason I see every experience as an opportunity to learn not just what to do, but what NOT to do. That way, next time you can deliver better results and grow.

> “If you’re not prepared to be wrong, you’ll never come up with anything original.”
>
> ***Sir Ken Robinson, The Element: How Finding Your Passion Changes Everything*** (16)

So that night after the boys were in bed, I reflected upon the ‘party chaos’ to figure out what I could do differently next time.

As a result, I created a system and a model based on nurturing children’s ideas – rather than encouraging them to make a specific something. And it worked! When I turned up at my next party I pulled out the ‘ideas box’ and handed out the ‘magic capes’ so the children could run around as superheroes, or whatever else they fancied.

We had wooden treasure chests to decorate and then clay to model and sculpt with. I also provided a third activity after the food. I supplied the party bags, which the children personalised and these were filled with the children’s own arty creations. I can remember the proud faces of the little ones as they clutched their bags and showed off their work to their parents. The party was a big hit and I remember going home that night and opening a bottle of wine to celebrate.

> "Around here, however, we don't look backwards for very long. We keep moving forward, opening up new doors and doing new things, because we're curious...and curiosity keeps leading us down new paths."
>
> ***Walt Disney Company***

Another challenge was to ensure the quality and standards of the products we used and supplied to franchisees to run classes and parties. Back in 2010, we outsourced the fulfilment of our arts and crafts products, but we had a number of problems managing deliveries to our franchise owners. It was a real dilemma.

At the time I was running the business from an office at home. I had twenty franchise owners and our garage, and increasingly our house, was gradually taken over by creative products. One day in particular stands out. I remember lining up twenty boxes on my drive and frantically packing them with sequins, buttons, glue, pipe cleaners, glitter, foam, card etc. and just hoping it didn't rain.

Then my hips got really bad again...

One day I walked into town and couldn't walk back. I was in so much pain I didn't know what was happening to me.

Despite numerous consultations, no one could figure out what was wrong. It was so frustrating because the problem was so unpredictable. It was 'a bit of a pickle' as they say. I couldn't even walk across the road and could no longer walk my kids to school.

Eventually I discovered something called 'Myofascial release'. It turned out that the running I'd started doing had created an imbalance in my muscles and ligaments. This treatment, thankfully, sorted me out – and I now go back every three months for a checkup. I look on it as an MOT, as it keeps me going.

As my legs got better I knew I'd come to a crossroads. With a rapidly growing business and the increased pressure on our home to cope with materials, it was clear we needed dedicated premises – a warehouse where we could take control of the products. It felt like a big decision and a huge step. I didn't want to work in an unattractive warehouse with no windows. I felt that it didn't fit our creative values. If I was going to leave home then I wanted to work somewhere beautiful that made my team and me feel good about working there.

Then there was the dilemma of vacating my home office. I'd started my business to be around for my children. If I had to work from an office, then I wouldn't be at home. It felt like a clash of values. But instinctively I knew with a bit of creative thinking the right solution would emerge.

I knew I had to adapt to the changing needs of my business. Fortunately, my brilliant sister, Fran had a great idea. "Why don't we get you a laptop then you can work in the office until 3pm and then go home with the kids."

It was the perfect compromise – that's the power of creative thinking. All that was left to do was find the right space, and The Creation Station could 'grow-up!'

I found our Creative Hub one day when out on a bike ride.

I stumbled across a barn conversion with warehouse facilities and in 2013 we moved in and spread out over two floors.

After a year, we outgrew our offices and were lucky to get some additional space in 2014. Then we outgrew our space yet again. In early 2016, the Dutch barn, or cow barn as we used to call it, was being converted into offices. So, we moved in and created the perfect working environment for us.

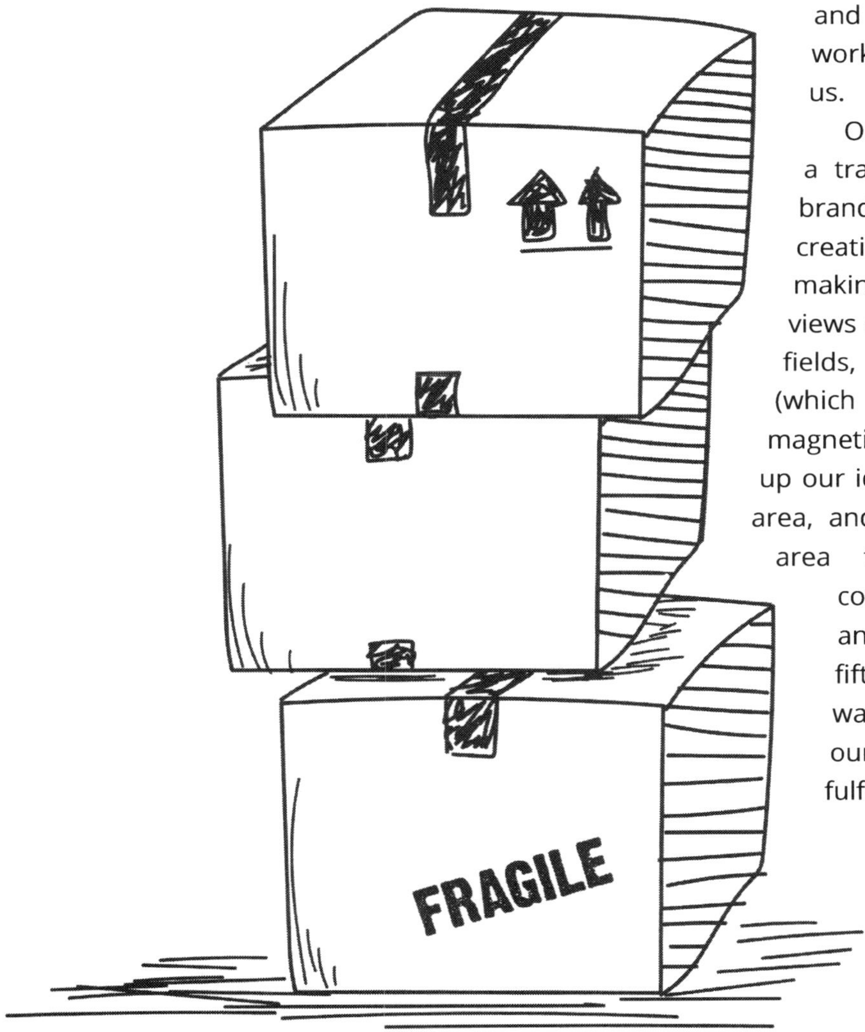

Our bespoke office has a training room with our brand values displayed, a creative area for testing, making and filming, stunning views over the Devon rolling fields, space for our awards (which is now pretty full), a magnetic orange wall to pin up our ideas, a print and post area, and an outdoor seating area for team meetings complete with coffee and cake. We are also fifteen steps from our warehouse, which makes our customer service and fulfilment so much easier.

And now time for you

'Failure' is part and parcel of life. For example, we accept that a baby will fall down when learning to walk and not everything will go to plan every time. As we get older we become more fearful of the consequences. If we're not careful, fear of failure can prevent us from grasping life and can mean we miss out on opportunities that our hearts really want.

It can be helpful to develop resilience. The ability to cope when things go wrong and to embrace the learning experience that setbacks present and not beat ourselves up for making a mistake. It's a valuable lesson to help your child to recognise that 'failure' is OK and lessons learnt are more powerful than what you learn from succeeding. But before you can do that you need to understand your own thoughts about failure.

When my children 'fail' I encourage them to feel the emotion. For example, if they are sad I don't change the subject, but encourage them to acknowledge the emotion and explain it's OK to feel this way. I ask open questions – to encourage them to talk about how they are feeling. Then finally, if it feels appropriate at the time, we talk about what they would do differently next time, or if there's anything they've learnt from the experience.

If children and adults are OK with failure, they'll be able to reflect and learn valuable life lessons. In turn, there's every chance they'll take the necessary risks to gain what they want in life.

How do you feel about failure? How do you support your child when things don't work out? Could you take more 'risks' to push your comfort zone. Use the space overleaf to ponder over these questions.

Raising a family with creative intelligence

From my collection of experiences, I've discovered that life is affected by many factors.

From risk taking, to self-belief, and the importance of resilience, these all help build the mental strength that help you bounce back when you hit tough times.

I feel incredibly fortunate to have been able to develop my passion for nurturing creativity. But as you can see the success of The Creation Station and my wider career is down to many factors. The greatest one being the people I've been privileged to meet, from my pretty awesome kids and husband, to my supportive family, great friends, incredible colleagues, inspiring customers, and so many stakeholders.

I'd do it all again...

Taking a creative approach to my life has opened doors for me that would otherwise have remained shut. I've had the privilege to travel, carve out my own path, and raise a family that shares my value of fun, curiosity, and expressing the wonder within.

It won't come as any surprise to hear that creative sparks and innovation are topics I'm passionate about! It's one of the reasons I feel so privileged to speak about these subjects. I've been the keynote speaker at women in business events and the British Franchise Association as well as networking groups, start-up business exhibitions, childcare exhibitions, and parenting and education events. My talks are always tailored to the group I am speaking with and have included:

- **Creative Sparks**
  Unleash the wonder within

- **Creativity and Innovation**
  A creative approach to business

It's always good to meet and talk with people I would have otherwise never met.

It's also great to see creativity incorporated in its wider perspective (i.e. not just about the arts but as an approach to living) and for these important topics to make the front cover of a mainstream magazine.

I was delighted to be asked to be the face on the front of Elite Franchise in March 2017. I enjoyed my interview for the main feature where I got to talk about how creativity led to franchising opportunities. The front cover captured me sitting on the fence in front of a field of maize – the view outside our offices.

bfa
AFFILIATE
elitefranchise
elitefranchisemagazine.co.uk
JUNE 2017 £4.50
Crolla's Gelateria
Franchising is breathing new life into the 122-year-old ice-cream company
The trailblazers
Why pioneers take the risk of becoming companies' first franchisees
Husse
How a lifelong animal lover brought the Swedish pet-food franchise to the UK
COVER STAR
COLOURING OUTSIDE THE LINES
16
Rather than teaching children that there's only one way to do things, with The Creation Station Sarah Cressall is using art to activate kids' imaginations

It's been a privilege to be in a position to impact upon other children and families through the power of creativity.

But I've also loved seeing how this approach to life has impacted upon my own kids. The boys were brought up to have a creative outlook as I felt this was the best way I could give them a framework to cope and thrive in life – and I hope it's paid off. A Sunday Telegraph journalist interviewed me recently about creative ideas and activities for kids. Our conversation turned to my boys and she asked if they were creative. "Absolutely," I said, "but not in the way you may think".

My boys enjoy sketching occasionally, but their creativity is most apparent when they're problem-solving science, maths, and programming challenges. Over the years, their maths teachers have all said that the boys are very good at seeing what isn't there. They can think around problems to find a range of solutions.

Creativity shows up in their communication skills too. The boys make good eye contact, confidently initiate conversations, and are genuinely interested in other people – whatever their age. These are the character traits that are noticed again and again by friends and people we don't know.

As well as developing their creative intelligence, I feel privileged they've been able to contribute to the growth of The Creation Station too. The boys have been involved since day one. Firstly, as participants, and as they got older, their ideas contributed to the development of our workshops. They've also all helped run workshops, parties, and events. Whenever we've created something new the boys have been involved.

The boys took charge of the photo session when Kirsty, a fantastic local childminder, brought her children to our house for a creative session (many of those photos are inside this book). That was a particularly magical moment for me. I loved seeing my boys getting stuck in and helping others be creative around our kitchen table. It was emotional because the creative spark for The Creation Station happened around our kitchen table back in 2002.

The boys voices are even captured on our first album. Our Little Explorer classes finish with a song called 'We are creative kids'. You may have heard of it? The talented John Meredith recorded this song when we lived in Loughborough. The kids sang it in their PJs because it was way past their bedtime.

My boys have all helped with developing and running Creation Station, from helping with classes and events, to organising stock, they have been a brilliant support.

I'm not sure if I was breaking any human rights, but they were well paid with cuddles and praise.

The fact that you can involve your kids and plan work around family commitments, is something that many of our franchise owners also value.

For me, it's meant I've been able to prioritise family commitments which has provided the best of both worlds.

It does mean that I have had to work late in the evening or get up early to get things done, but I do feel I've benefited from having choice and control over my working hours.

I've asked my kids over the years how they have felt about being so involved with Creation Station and if it had made any difference to them. Their comments have been around appreciating how different everyone is and knowing it was OK to feel different and not always 'fit in'. They talked about growing in confidence, thinking out of the box and not just going with the first answer but exploring other ideas.

Like any parent, I'm super proud of my kids – they are all very different, but they are kind, thoughtful and have great social skills. I think these are pretty good attributes to help them to to cope with and hopefully make the most of, life's unknown adventures.

In many ways, we've all benefited from having a business that blends with our family. After all, running a business has many similarities to being a parent. You need to set and live by the standards you want your family to adopt. Just like in business. It helps when you have a clear purpose and vision because it's less likely that things will change on a whim and you avoid mixed messages. When you lack clarity about what's important, things get miscommunicated. We all know kids push boundaries. They need to do this to see how much give they're allowed. So being clear and sticking to your principles helps everyone. That said, as your kids grow and life changes, it's important to listen to them and compromise where appropriate.

Just like with employees.

When you empower people to make their own decisions, they feel more invested in the outcome. I find this with my own team. I believe everyone is capable of doing a great job. My role is to support them to do that with clear goals and the tools, resources and support they need. It's the same with my kids. I believe they are great and are very capable. My role is to support them to live a healthy, happy and fulfilled life.

When you support each other, you get the best from each other. It's one of the reasons why my husband was able to fulfil a lifelong dream recently. Ever since I met him back in 1991, he's talked about sailing across the Atlantic. He didn't do it at the time, and when the kids were little the timing wasn't right for us as a family.

Fast-forward to 2017 and things came together.

2017 was a big year for us - 20 years married, 15 years of running The Creation Station, and a 'significant' birthday for me. When an opportunity arose for Duncan to take part in the Clipper Race, we grabbed it.

The Clipper Race is a round-the-world race established by Sir Robin Knox Johnson BVE who himself sailed single-handedly around the world in 1968/1969 . He wanted to give other people, novice sailors, the opportunity to experience this extreme adventure. He set up the Clipper Race. This is where twelve, seventy-foot boats, race across the world stopping in eight countries during an eleven-month sail.

We discussed Duncan's participation as a family and worked through the implications of him being away for over three months. The kids' first reaction was to say, 'OMG that sounds fantastic but the house will be a mess!' Duncan sorts all kinds of things at home, but we decided we could step up to the challenge. The university where Duncan works doing facilities management also kindly agreed to a three-months' sabbatical. Once he'd completed the selection procedure, had to undertake four separate weeks of training. While Duncan had sailed a bit as a kid, that was a long time ago and each week seemed to get tougher and tougher.

Before we knew it, it was time for the race to start and on Friday 18th August, the whole family travelled to Liverpool to wave him off. That's me and the boys, Duncan's twin brother Andrew, his wife Toni, and their children, his sister Isobel, husband Chris and one of their kids Will.

The journey was a long eight hours from Devon, but we had the perfect distraction. If you don't use this on long journeys already, I hope this one tip will be worth you buying this book! With the help of Fran, we downloaded a great audio book which was eight and a half hours long.

We were all so engrossed in the sci-fi adventure that the journey flew by.

My mum joined us on the Sunday morning and we all stood at the dock watching the twelve magnificent boats sail out to sea. As I noticed the 45 degree tilt I finally understood why Duncan had said that life on the boat was physically hard work. At sea he'd have to cope with a wide range of pressures whilst crammed into a small lower deck with twenty other crew. They had to share bunk beds too and would take shifts of four or six hours on and off.

As I watched him set sail to Uruguay I was part excited, part terrified, and a bit sad too. I was going to miss him, and not just because he puts the bins out on a Wednesday. It was to be the longest we've been apart since we first met.

We agreed we wouldn't see him in Uruguay, but the boys and I planned to see him finish the race in Cape Town which as luck would have it coincided with October half-term.

But then I had a bit of a mad idea. I decided I could pop out and see him in Uruguay!

That's one of the best things about building such a capable, committed, passionate team. I had complete confidence they'd be able to do the planned training for our new franchise owners while I was away.

But I'd never left the kids alone...

I knew they were old enough, but it was still a major concern. I was going to be away for ten nights and that felt like a long time. My boys have lots of friends and as I thought back to my own teenage years, I wondered what chaos I'd return to. We sat together and discussed my concerns with them. I explained if they couldn't look after themselves, each other, and our home, I couldn't go. They were brilliant and promised me they'd be OK and that I should go and see dad.

Four days before I flew out, Duncan had just arrived into Punte Del Este, Uruguay. I FaceTimed him and he was really tired. It had been a tough trip, but he'd survived and thrived. Then I asked him if he wanted to go to dinner in four days, his face was a picture and I knew we'd made the right decision.

We had a brilliant time and even went to Buenos Aires for a long weekend. We did a bicycle tour of the urban and street art and another tour into the heart of the city. If you've not experienced a cycling tour I highly recommend it. You get a real feel for the area and cover a lot of ground too. We particularly enjoyed seeing the urban art as it's often the portrayal of the pulse of the city, the heart, the struggles and their unique culture.

We returned to Uruguay and Duncan had a few days of work to do in the boat before setting off for Cape Town. I had some work to do and was also finishing this book.

Unfortunately, I was quite poorly and ended up in bed for two days. I then had a pretty long journey home and a very dodgy tummy. One of my flight connections was cancelled and so I was delayed for a day. Not ideal but although I felt awful, I did recognise that I was also happy. I think this got me through.

One of the great things about going away is arriving back home. It was wonderful to see the boys. The house was spotless, the lawn, or more of a grassy muddy patch, had been mown and the laundry was put away in everyone's room. We'd FaceTimed whilst I was away, so Duncan and I had seen what they were doing, but I was stunned to see how much they'd stepped up. Duncan and I were so proud, but what was even lovelier was to see how proud they were of themselves and each other.

It was an important lesson for me. Believing in your kids and giving them the opportunity to step up is very worthwhile. They can surprise you too. The boys even managed to fix the broken dishwasher by phoning customer service (I didn't even know it had customer service!) What's more, they continued to cook and sort things out for a few more days after my return, so I could recover fully from my dodgy tummy.

In family life, as in business, we don't always get it right. But if you live with personal integrity you can learn from setbacks, cope when things go wrong, and maximise the ups when things go right.

And now time for you

What steps could you take to help you take to help your child develop their creative intelligence?

Putting creativity back into childhood

A creative approach is something that can infuse through all areas of life. And as parents, we have a fantastic opportunity to introduce our children to new ideas, experiences, and concepts. Remember, if the core of creativity is about making connections, the more children have to draw on and the more their imagination can explore.

This principle has always been at the heart of The Creation Station experience. We're all about giving children the opportunity to develop their creative intelligence.

And it's been an absolute joy, so much fun, and incredibly rewarding to build something that has touched such a rich diversity of people.

I'm proud to say that from the single class I started in 2002 (just after my youngest son Josh was born), The Creation Station has grown to help inspire over 16,000 children families and adults with classes, parties and events every week across the UK. We do this through our portfolio of creative experiences including:

- **Tiny Treasures** – crafty keepsakes for newborns to six months and Tiny Treasures for nurseries where we create craft keepsakes with the children and provide nurseries with free crafts
- **Baby Discover**, **Little Explorer**, and **Family Fun** sessions for children aged 6 months to 11 years
- **Arty Parties** and **Event Entertainment**
- Out of school **Create Clubs** and **creative school workshops**
- **Creative Crafters** – fun, creative sessions for adults
- **Care and Creativity** – creative workshops designed for adults after designed for senior citizens, which often takes place in care homes and health centres. Plus our **intergenerational workshops** where we bring our older and younger generations together, to enjoy creative fun together.

Our product range had expanded to over 13,000 arts and crafts products and we've even launched a product that has the potential to put The Creation Station philosophy into every home through our FAB Boxes.

Each FAB Box includes ten activities plus ten ideas to inspire young minds. They are designed for children aged five to eleven and due to demand, we now provide them on a monthly subscription. In addition, we're developing this into a FAB project. Every time one FAB box is purchased, we donate crafts to a child or group in need.

> "Imagination is the beginning of creation. You imagine what you desire, you will what you imagine and at last you create what you will."
>
> ***George Bernard Shaw***

We've been fortunate to have been recognised by a number of awards too, including:

- Voted 5-Star in an independent Franchise satisfaction survey in 2018, 2017, and 2016.
- Best Website 2017 in the National Franchise Awards
- Franchisee of the Year Award in the British Franchise Association awards 2017 – **Ruth Morris** won this very prestigious award
- Winner Excellence and Innovation, Children's Education Services 2017
- Finalist Richard Branson's Impact Award 2016
- Winner Best Creative Play Award 2015
- Finalist Festival Supplier Awards 2015
- Winner Entrepreneur of the Year 2013
- Finalist Business Woman Of The Year 2012

- Winner Best Woman Franchisor UK 2011 – EWIF Awards
- Winner Best Franchisee Marketing Support 2012
- Winner 'Crème de la Crème' Business Award 2011
- Winner 'Best Interactive Business' Award – Mumpreneur 2011
- Finalist 'Extraordinary Woman of the Year' 2011
- Business Woman of the Year 2009 – Women of Achievement Awards Leicestershire

It's been an amazing journey so far. At times I feel as though we're still at the tip of the iceberg, or jelly as we say. And that's why I'm excited about what's coming next...

Some of our newer projects – including partnerships with bigger brands – really kicked off after 2012, when I decided to stop running classes myself and focus on putting creativity on the map.

Our growing network of franchise owners proved the model worked. I needed to free up my time so I could focus on supporting and nurturing new and existing franchise owners to help them achieve the success they want.

For the last five years, I've focused my attention on leading the Creative Hub head office team, based in Devon. Together, we help and support 130 franchise owners from across the UK – many of whom are mums, dads, and grandparents.

Then in 2017, we celebrated The Creation Station's 15th anniversary at our annual Inspiring Imaginations conference in Cadbury House Hotel, Bristol. It seemed a fitting acknowledgment to my chocolate inspired daydreams as a kid!

It was wonderful to have so many of our franchise owners there, many of whom have shared The Creation Station journey for over eight years. Our theme was the glitter challenge designed to raise funds for UNICEF to help brighten up children's lives. It was an honour to have Debra Searle MVO MBE talk about her single-handed row across the Atlantic. I was thrilled that Duncan and the kids could make the evening celebrations and they gave out the awards with a huge amount of funny banter and grace.

Thinking big, I've also set new goals. For example, we're keen to explore more partnerships with brands that are aligned with our values – similar to the Hasbro Play-Doh and Lego-Duplo partnerships and the work we've done with Aardman and Sony in recent times.

I'm also open to ideas and suggestions. For me, it's all about empowering children with the power of creativity and showing them what's possible when you enhance your creative intelligence.

We had a huge amount of momentum behind our campaign to put creativity back into childhood. In 2016, we entered Richard Branson's Pitch to Rich competition. Out of 5,000 companies we were one of three finalists in the Impact category.

We are working with experts to develop effective programmes and have started a roll-out with our Care & Creativity workshops. It's an area which is in great need of support and we are keen to help where we can.

I'm enormously proud of the support of the team, colleagues, friends and family to help us inspire imaginations and nurture creativity to bring outcomes in all our lives.

I truly believe, as do our team that creativity can change the world.

We've inspired

950,000

children, families and adults so far,

but that's only the tip of the iceberg.

I'm driven to make a difference and I want to do that by inspiring more people with the power of creativity. I'm approaching this challenge in a number of ways.

I'm delighted to be one of the founders of the Children's Activity Association. Our objectives are twofold. Firstly, we'll work with other professional children's activity businesses and professionals to give parents a benchmark for all organised children's activities. The association will achieve this by establishing and improving standards and accreditation. Secondly, our aim is to give more children the opportunity to experience a wider range of organised activities.

We'd also like to bring creative arts and crafts to more children. To do that I need to find more like-minded people to help. It's why we're aiming to create a further 100 new franchise opportunities in the UK.

I don't know exactly when I'll achieve this target simply because I don't know how long it will take us to find the right people. I'm aiming for two to three years, but I won't compromise on the enthusiasm and fit of people who join our community.

I'm passionate and proud about our values. They infuse through everything we do and help to keep us focused on making a difference. What this has meant is that we do attract people who care about these things too. We have a phenomenal team, both at Creative Hub and across the UK. I hadn't envisaged the calibre of the people I would work with – I think it's one of the best things about our business, not just the children we are privileged to share creative journeys with, but also the people we work with.

I do know that there are still lots of creative adventures ahead and while this may be The Creation Station's story so far, there are plenty more chapters to be written in the future.

And we'd love you to play a part.

Whether that's by trying some of the activities included in the book (at home or work), by joining a class or experience near you, or even running your own flexible and rewarding Creation Station franchise.

You can discover more about nurturing your child's creativity in the next section. And if you'd like to know what Creation Station activities are happening near you, simply visit **www.thecreationstation.co.uk**

So now that I've shared my story, let's explore yours.

A creative outlook has the potential to open so many doors for you and your children, just as it has for me and my family. Let's continue onto Part 2 and understand why creativity matters.

I think you'll find it eye-opening...

Characters we now use inspired by the original dudes in my comic.

Part 2

Why creativity matters

Why creativity matters

As parents, we strive to do our best for our children. For me, my hope is to give my three boys what they need to live a happy and fulfilled life.

I'm sure I'm not alone in this thinking. In fact, I believe this is every parent's dream – but how can we make it a reality for our children? Especially because the pressure is on.

As you know time passes so fast and children grow up so quickly. In fact, blink and before we know it our kids will be adults at the driving force of our society, our economy, our culture, and our future.

It could be a rough journey. As you know, the children of today face challenges and pressures that are vastly different to a generation ago. Today's world is incredibly fast-paced and more connected than ever before. With information at our fingertips, social media at the heart of conversations, and geographical boundaries fragmenting, the 'norms' are changing all the time. As our societies become more diverse we seem to have trouble embracing the change and are fearful of the implications. Perhaps this is one of the reasons why there is an increase in stress, destruction, and mental health issues.

As a result, there's uncertainty, peer pressure, and a push for conformity supported by an education system that insists on assessing talent based on performance in exams. Economic change has caused big upheavals too. The 'job for life' our parents enjoyed no longer exists.

Now micro businesses lead the way as traditional industries struggle, and many seek out flexible ways to mix parenting with enterprise.

In reality, it's no surprise that family life has come under increased pressure too. Parents work longer hours meaning quality family time is harder to create. Alongside this, childhood experiences and traditions are shifting as screen time increasingly replaces outdoor play and children are fast-tracked into adult worlds arguably too quickly.

In the light of all these challenges and the underlying tone of negativity, uncertainty, and fear... how can we best equip children to cope in this fast-paced, ever-changing world? What can we do to help them make the right decisions, create solutions, and make the world a better place?

I believe that creativity, creative intelligence, and the creative process holds the key. It's why I'm so committed to put creativity back into childhood

And in the pages that follow I'll explain why.

Creativity unlocks potential

I find it hugely frustrating that the true value of creativity is often misunderstood and overlooked. For me, developing your child's creative intelligence is just as important as teaching them to count or swim. That's because creativity is a fundamental life skill that will empower the next generation to survive and thrive in our ever-changing world.

That's because, at its core, a creative mindset and outlook can help your child know who they are.

Creativity helps to define their identity. It celebrates their uniqueness. It helps to unlock the wonder within so that your child can become the person they are 'meant' to be.

Without a creative outlook you're more likely to conform to the accepted norm. You blend in. You'll stifle your uniqueness and you may struggle to adapt and find your place in society. In fact, I believe if people don't have a creative outlook or outlet in their lives it can cause emotional pain – because all that potential is left untapped and locked away.

If you can't be your true self, then you can feel that you don't belong.

But creativity offers an alternative...

It can help us to feel in control of who we are and what we become. When we express our ideas, and explore our creative talents we develop enormously.

And there's a huge amount of research to back this up. For example, creative activities have been proven to help develop important personality traits such as curiosity, self-motivation, self-confidence, and the ability to tolerate ambiguity. Exploring creative activities can also help develop emotional processes such as emotional fantasy in play, pleasure in challenge, involvement in tasks, and tolerance of anxiety (17).

But that's not all... Parents are always surprised when they discover the depth of learning their child can enjoy as a result of engaging in creative arts and crafts at our sessions.

Here's a list of some of the benefits... Children are able to:

- Compare different materials
- Develop their own ideas
- Share with others
- Sort and organise information
- Analyse information
- Appreciate beauty
- Give attention to detail
- Be more aware of how to stay safe
- Experience the world through their different senses
- Feel happier
- Break away from stereotypes
- Bond with each other
- Develop their communication skills, concentration, and determination
- Feel confident eating healthy foods and trying new experiences and activities
- Be bolder with their creative expression
- Embrace diversity
- Envision solutions
- Express themselves
- Find their voice
- Develop their hand-eye coordination, fine motor skills, and hand and finger strength

- Have and express their own opinion
- Investigate and innovate
- Learn from their mistakes
- Become better listeners
- Make choices and decisions that are right for them
- Make connections between information and ideas
- Develop their mark-making and writing skills
- Explore through movement and balance and develop spatial awareness
- Enhance their observation skills
- Show patience, persistence and perseverance
- Solve problems
- Develop social skills as they learn to share, respect others, and develop relationships
- Reflect on their work and self-evaluate
- See another point of view
- Develop self-confidence and self-esteem
- Start a dialogue
- Think
- Understand that an object can exist even when out of sight
- Understand the concept of large and small
- Understand that they can affect their environment
- Understand the world around them
- Experiment with materials
- Value aesthetics

What's even more interesting is this list is supported by our own research too. We surveyed the parents who come to our classes to ask them to describe how they think their children benefit. Here's a collection of feedback:

See over 2,000 more great reviews on our site - www.thecreationstation.co.uk

Caroline Bergeron
Published on Trustpilot 24.10.17

Brilliant

I really enjoy attending Creation Station with my 13 month old son. Charlotte is so lovely, friendly and organised! It's great to have something different to take home each week that I can display at home, including precious items such as my son's footprint in clay. I have especially enjoyed exploring autumn colours and textures this term. There have been lots of interesting sensory experiences for the babies to discover like slippery spaghetti and sticky surfaces. It's a brilliant class that I'd recommend to anyone with young children.

Tina Thompson
Published on Trustpilot 24.04.18

We had a great evening doing different...

We had a great evening doing different crafts , a lovely way to unwind and relax whilst trying something new. Would definitely recommend and Emma our tutor was knowledgeable and a bubbly lady who made it fun. ☺ ☺ ☺

Megan Jones
Published on Trustpilot 16.04.18

A Fantastic Party by Creation Station

Jen from Creation Station ran our children's party - a joint party for our son and daughter who were turning 5 and 7. The party was fantastic and catered to all the ages. Jen had a lovely way with the kids, she was very well organised and the activities were great - the whole party from start to finish was fantastic and the kids all loved it (and the grown ups!) I couldn't recommend Jen and Creation Station enough - thanks Jen!

Lisa
Published on Trustpilot 12.04.18

Great activities for all 3 of my...

Great activities for all 3 of my children so much fun and they can't wait to go again. Good value for money.

Claire Johnson
Published on Trustpilot 10.04.18

My boys had a fab time today.

My boys had a fab time today! Total bargain for the price and really well organised. We hadn't even left and 3 year old was asking when we were going again! Thank you xx

What does it mean to be creative?

If creativity encourages the development of so many skills, why is this characteristic not embraced and taught as standard in schools?

Why is creativity not an intrinsic and critical part of childhood?

I believe this is a complex issue and there's not one clear answer. For example, you could argue that it's not easy for schools to nurture creativity. After all, there's a lack of time and resources to allow all children the freedom to discover their own way. Teaching within more restricted boundaries is more trackable and there's an argument that as a collective you get more done.

In addition, I think there's confusion over what it means to be creative. Somehow we've come to associate creativity as being good at drawing or excelling at music, literature, or the arts. And if we as adults don't perceive ourselves as creative, we don't give it our full attention.

But artistic talent provides a limited understanding of what it means to be creative. The dictionary definition gets us a little closer:

noun

The use of imagination or original ideas to create something; inventiveness.

If creativity is about inventiveness and the use of imagination, then it follows that creativity is at work in all aspects of education and life – including the more analytical subjects such as science, technology, and mathematics.

In short, a creative approach to life is more widespread than you might think.

Broadening the definition still further, I believe creativity is about making connections and thinking differently. Steve Jobs said in a 1996 interview for Wired that:

> "Creativity is just connecting things. When you ask creative people how they did something, they feel a little guilty because they didn't really do it, they just saw something. It seemed obvious to them after a while. That's because they were able to connect experiences they've had and synthesize new things."
>
> ***Steve Jobs, Apple Inc***
> (18)

Other people have defined creativity as follows:

"Being creative enables children to make connections between one area of learning and another and so extend their understanding..."

Caroline Sharp
(19)

"Creativity is intelligence having fun."

Albert Einstein

"Creativity is inventing, experimenting, growing, taking risks, breaking rules, making mistakes, and having fun."

Mary Lou Cook

Taking inspiration from these definitions you can see that creativity, in its broadest sense, is about:

- Using our imagination
- Drawing upon our own resources to solve problems
- Working out fixes and inventing solutions
- Having the self-confidence to have a go and explore your ideas
- Creating something new that didn't previously exist
- Being resourceful
- Thinking without constraints or restraints
- Finding your own answers
- Expressing your inner thoughts
- Harnessing your natural curiosity
- Listening to your subconscious or your intuition

In short, creativity is a natural human trait.

The ability to be creative is in all of us – and you probably draw upon your creative ideas more than you realise. Think about it... We're always using our thinking and problem-solving skills to decide how to behave or react to ordinary events. In fact, we're required to 'think out of the box' to work around the most simplistic of situations.

For example:

Juggling your time so you can be in two places at once – almost! Answering your children's really challenging questions, while rustling up a meal with the three ingredients left in your fridge

You see creativity isn't restricted to those in the creative arts, but a skill we should all associate with and embrace, because we have it in abundance. As Maya Angelou so beautifully says:

> "You can't use up creativity. The more you use, the more you have."
>
> ***Maya Angelou***
> (20)

And if we were to all express our creativity, how different our world would be...

Creativity makes our world a better place

Despite the turmoil and change that's happening all around us, amazing innovations have helped society progress in the last few decades.

And creative thought has been at the heart of these changes. Think Anita Roddick, Steve Jobs, Richard Branson, and Mark Zuckerberg, to name just a few. These creative minds broke the mould, changed how we thought, and introduced new 'normals'.

For example, Roddick challenged our views about animal testing, Branson showed that a newcomer could transform an industry, and Jobs and Zuckerberg revolutionised human behaviour and changed the way we communicate.

Although wildly different, all these innovations had one thing in common… they all started out as an idea in someone's head – a fleeting belief, a thought, a daydream… the notion that something could be different or better.

These individuals are proof that a creative thought can be transformed into something real and tangible. That something small can become mighty, and even when a goal seems ridiculously unachievable, it's amazing what the human mind has the capacity to do when an unshakeable self-belief is coupled with a creative spirit.

> “If you think you’re too small to have an impact, try going to bed with a mosquito.”
>
> ***Anita Roddick***
> (21)

These individuals pushed against conformity because they saw a different way.

And here’s the thing… if these individuals were able to achieve great things, then why not your children? Why not you?

It’s a fact that we all have unlimited potential…

Children are proof of this. If you’ve been around young children, you’ll know they’re free thinkers and creative beings instinctively. They believe they can be an astronaut, a ballerina, or a racing driver, or a unicorn for example. After all, anything is possible in a small child’s imagination because their thinking isn’t limited or inhibited by the more ‘sensible’, ‘rational’, ‘judgemental’, and ‘practical’ thoughts we have as grown-ups.

> “Imagination is more important than knowledge. For knowledge is limited to all we now know and understand, while imagination embraces the entire world, and all there ever will be to know and understand.”
>
> ***Albert Einstein***

But sadly, this instinctive creativity and unrestricted imagination doesn’t seem to last into adulthood and I believe there’s an urgent need to reverse this trend.

Let me explain...

Formal education doesn't always help

Evidence suggests that we are all born with some characteristics that are genetically determined.

These innate skills help to shape our character and determine who we are, but nurture also plays a crucial role in our development. Whilst it's true that some people are more naturally creative than others, that doesn't mean you can't enhance your creative intelligence.

In fact, creativity can be nurtured and developed when you give it attention, encouragement and freedom. The problem is that creativity is often unwittingly stifled through continuous monitoring, evaluation, adult-direction, and the pressure to conform.

Our experiences and beliefs can influence our expectations about what is, and isn't possible for us to the extent that we dumb down a creative response. And whilst logical thinking can help our decision-making, without creativity, the breadth of ideas is limited.

Interestingly, evidence suggests that creativity appears to decline from about the age of five. Now this may be coincidental, but this is also the age when children begin their formal educational journey here in the UK.

We know that people in the education system do a fantastic job.

There are many incredibly passionate and exceptionally skilled teachers and childcare professionals who work tirelessly to support, nurture, and educate children. However, sometimes their hands can be tied by constraints they can't change.

I strongly believe that we can't rely on schools alone to develop children's creativity. In fact, I talk with a lot of teachers who tell me they feel the increased level of paperwork has taken away from them the time and energy available to focus on teaching and helping children.

A colleague retold this story to me and it's similar to countless other stories I've heard.

"It was the end of term and all the children seemed quite tired, there was half an hour to go until home time so I decided to read them a story.

The children gathered round and as I finished the story the classroom door opened. The head walked in and asked me where was my lesson plan for that activity. I explained that I didn't have one - I changed the activity as the children all seemed very tired, and it wasn't long to go until they went home.

I was told in no uncertain terms that I could never do that again. The children were five years of age. That was the day when I decided to leave teaching after 20 years"

Of course we need to structure education in schools. We need a way of measuring performance and results, but if I was the mummy to one of those children, I know which activity I would have preferred the teacher to do.

The pressure on schools, and on the dedicated and hard-working teachers, teaching assistants and support staff, makes it increasingly difficult to devote quality time to nurture individual growth. There's a curriculum to follow, targets to hit, and league tables to consider. As a result, classroom activities must fit within particular parameters meaning less scope for individuality and more focus on standardised achievement.

"The fact is that given the challenges we face, education doesn't need to be reformed -- it needs to be transformed. The key to this transformation is not to standardise education, but to personalise it, to build achievement on discovering the individual talents of each child, to put students in an environment where they want to learn and where they can naturally discover their true passions."

Sir Ken Robinson, The Element: How Finding Your Passion Changes Everything

To be honest, I do find this standardised approach in schools rather peculiar. More and more we are subjecting children to an educational system that assumes one right answer to every question and one correct solution to every problem. It's like a sausage machine.

I think this needs to change...

Children need opportunities to express their individuality

Instead of allowing rational thought to rule, we need to keep creativity in the mix – because that's where the fresh ideas and new approaches come from.

> "I never made one of my discoveries through the process of rational thinking."
>
> ***Albert Einstein***
> (16)

A standardised approach to education stifles creative thinking hugely. What's more, a child's confidence can be knocked if their ideas don't fit with the accepted 'norm'. Perhaps this is why many children can become frustrated at school – and with life.

This could also be the reason that some gifted children or individuals with strong personalities don't achieve their potential at school. They may feel like a 'round peg in a square hole'. They feel different because they don't 'blend in' or think like everybody else. And this is a problem... I've found that when children feel the need to conform to certain expectations, their identity can be suppressed. For example, they may stop speaking out, they may dumb down their ideas, they may even stop trying. And even if the individual is not consciously aware of the impact, I believe their subconscious is.

Other children can struggle with the academic demands of our education system simply because they lack the cognitive skills needed to process information and excel academically. Nowadays there's so much focus on the 'academics'. Modern apprenticeships are giving vocational qualifications a fresh face and this is good because not everyone is a bookworm who enjoys studying. Some people are naturally more hands on and learn by doing.

As a result, if they're not able to use their natural skills it's understandable why some children can find schoolwork and social situations more challenging than others.

This reminds me of a wonderful story that Sir Ken Robinson tells, which puts this into perspective. He describes a girl who wasn't doing very well at school. She was fidgeting and just not focussing in class.

Her mum took her to see a child psychologist to find out what could be done. The child's psychologist turned the radio on, took the mum out of the room, and said, "Let's watch and see what happens." Whilst they were watching, and out of view of the little girl, she started to dance.

The psychologist said, "There's nothing wrong with your daughter. She is a dancer." That little girl went on to head up the choreography at Sadler's Wells.

I think this story says it all, doesn't it? Just because a child doesn't excel at traditional academic subjects doesn't mean their unique talents are any less valuable. We just need to help children discover what they're really good at – and then help them develop that unique wonder within.

Interestingly, for children where school doesn't bring out the best in them, additional schoolwork or special attention won't address the underlying problem necessarily. Giving them more of the same academic approach can simply compound the frustration and intensify the social or learning difficulties they experience.

The race to nurture creativity

I don't know what lies ahead for our kids, but I do know that the future is uncertain. It's the reason I believe we need more positive, creative influences in our world.

And that journey can start now – because it's never too late to help your children develop their creativity. But your child's journey starts with you – because your influence is critical. And that's why here at The Creation Station we aim to empower parents to inspire and nurture their child's creativity.

We focus on arts and crafts because this is a proven, affordable, flexible vehicle that allows children to explore their imagination, build their self-confidence, and bring a new reality into the world. At the age of three or six a child may create an image that appears to an onlooker to be an indecipherable picture – but in the future that creative expression could generate the idea that defines a generation.

I'll explain some simple things that you can do to nurture your child's creativity in the next chapter. We aren't talking rocket science here and I'm sure you're probably already doing some of these instinctively. And although it isn't rocket science, it could of course lead to new innovations in rocket science!

And now time for you

What steps could you take to help you take to help your child develop their creative intelligence?

Part 3

A parent's role in nurturing creativity

A parent's role in nurturing creativity

The evidence is compelling – a focus on creativity can help children develop in tremendous and broad ways. And that's why I believe more time should be devoted to exploring and enhancing children's creative intelligence.

In fact, I believe where the nature of formal education can place restrictions on creative expression, it's our opportunity – as parents – to create an environment where imagination and creativity can flourish. In fact, parents and carers are in the perfect position to do this because you can tailor and personalise experiences and activities to suit the needs, talents, and interests of your child.

You don't have to follow a curriculum or achieve particular standards. Instead you can give your child the space to discover their own wonder within.

Even if you believe you don't have a creative bone in your body.

"The game is changing. It isn't just about math and science anymore. It's about creativity, imagination and, above all, innovation."

Business Week Magazine
(23)

If I'm not creative, how can I help my child?

In the years since I started running The Creation Station, I've met many parents who felt they weren't in a position to nurture their child's creativity – simply because they didn't believe they were creative.

But here's the crux...

You DON'T need to be creative to bring out the best in your child, although I have a sneaky suspicion you're far more creative than you give yourself credit for.

That's because the best way to nurture your child's creativity is to give them a safe, encouraging space where they can explore their imagination – without fear of judgement.

It's their ideas you want to unlock. This isn't about you teaching them. Instead it's about encouraging them to explore who they are.

In this way, your role is to give children opportunities that spark their imagination and curiosity – and then see what they do. On top of this, you need to resist the temptation to intervene if they don't do things the way you would – or if you think they're making a mistake, unless they're in danger of course.

Finally, as you unleash your child's imagination and creative spark, be ready to celebrate their achievements. Give feedback about what they've done well and encourage your child to talk about their creations. This positive reinforcement of who they are and what they've done will boost your child's confidence no end.

And remember... this is much easier to do than you think. Once you get going, you'll quickly gain confidence and momentum and I have some tips and techniques to help support you coming up soon.

I don't have the time

I'm a parent myself. While my boys are at the age where they're a little more independent, they still need me. I understand how hectic and pressured everyday life can be – especially when you're juggling children and other commitments.

Before you start worrying about how you can fit all this in let me reassure you, your child's creative education needn't take a lot of extra work or time.

Sure, there are structured arts and crafts activities that you can explore and I've provided 52 suggestions in Part 4 of this book. But there are also countless ideas and activities that you can weave into your everyday life – with ease.

In fact, the ad hoc, impromptu learning experiences are potentially even more valuable than structured time because they encourage your child to make creativity a way of life – not just something they do at the weekend.

Let me explain how this approach works...

Stimulate their senses

> "I hear and I forget. I see and I remember. I do and I understand."
>
> ***Confucius***

We all know learning has more effect when we're able to 'discover' something new for ourselves – rather than just being told. For example, imagine trying to explain to a child that when you touch a table with your bare fingers you leave no marks, but if you touch with paint, you'll transfer paint from your fingers onto the table.

This information is hard to grasp – until you see it with your own eyes. In fact, you'll want to see this with your own eyes so you can test the truth of the statement.

And that's the power of doing – it helps children to discover and learn for themselves.

This is one of the reasons why arts and crafts offer such huge learning opportunities. Rather than being a passive observer, children get fully involved in the activity. What's more, arts and crafts by their nature tend to be multisensory.

But what does this have to do with creativity?

Remember, creativity is about connecting things – because when we connect things in new and distinct ways, we create something fresh. Sure, not all connections will 'work' and some connections will turn out better than others.

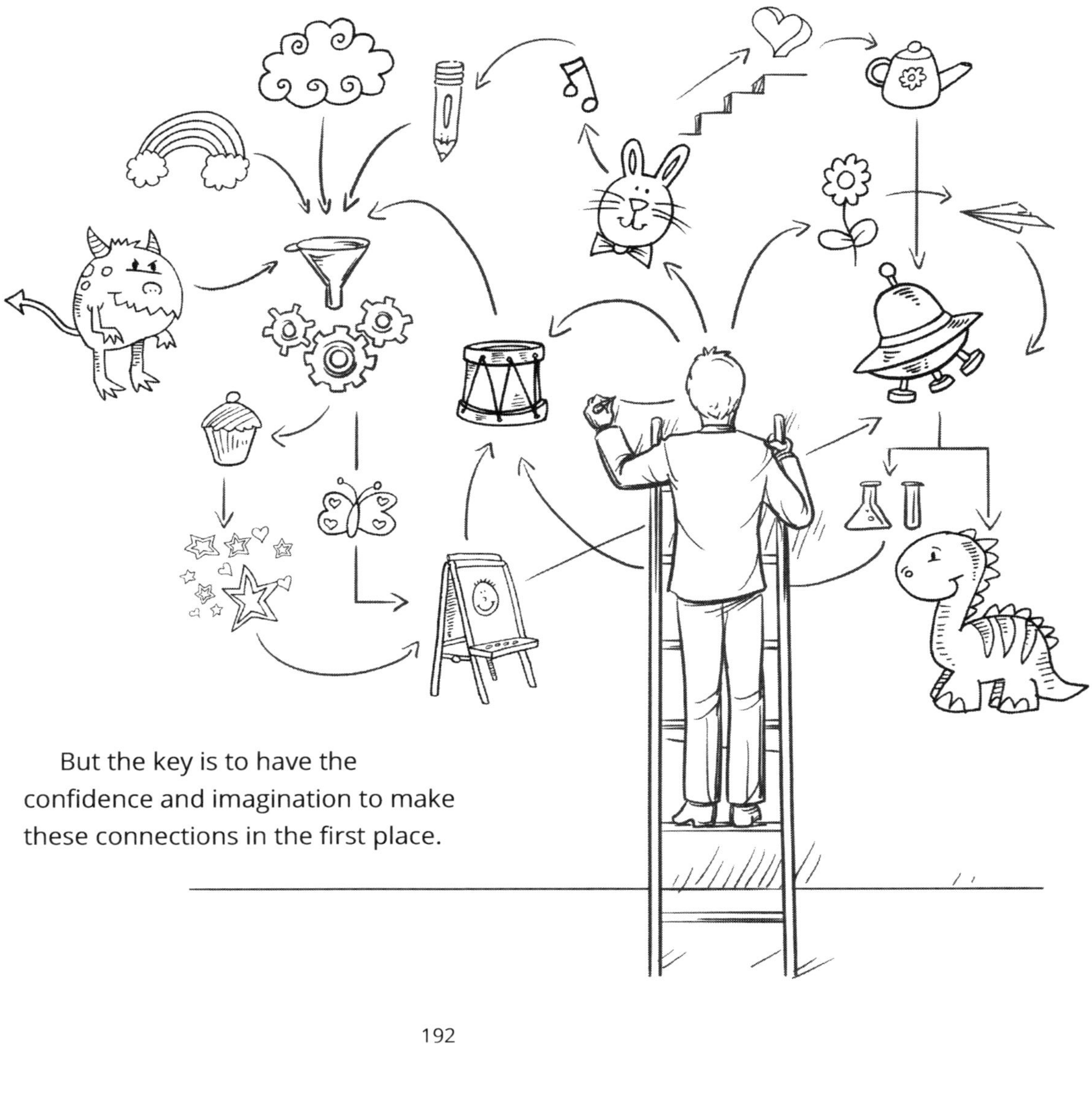

But the key is to have the confidence and imagination to make these connections in the first place.

Because every time we create something – we learn.

The more references, experiences, ideas, and materials we have at our disposal to connect up, the more expressive and experimental we can be with our creative ideas.

This is why sensory information is so key – because it helps us to build up a bank of 'things' that could be connected at a later date.

Let's explore this in more detail...

As you know, senses are the body's way of collecting information from the world around us. From sensory information, including smells, textures, temperature, sounds, tastes, and sights, as well as learning, children get to use all sorts of skills including:

- **Evaluation** – form an idea about something
- **Analysis** – understanding objects, situations, events in more detail
- **Memory** – I've seen that before
- **Making comparisons** – this is bigger than that
- **Understanding cause and effect** – if I put that on top it will squash what's underneath

And all the while, they are making sense of the world around them whilst increasing their knowledge and ideas.

All 'raw materials' waiting to be connected creatively.

So you see... when you stimulate a child's senses you nurture their creativity by default. And as you know, the opportunities to explore sensory experiences are huge. Just go and play at the beach, the forest, or by the river and your senses will go into overdrive.

See how simple it is to nurture a child's creativity? Simply provide situations where their senses are stimulated.

Now most of us are familiar with the five senses. But did you know there are at least eight? (And most researchers think there are around twenty-one.)

Here are the main eight senses:

1. **Sight** – we see with our eyes
2. **Auditory** – we hear with our ears
3. **Smell** – we smell with our nose
4. **Taste** – we taste with our mouth
5. **Tactile** – we touch with our hands – in fact, the whole of our body
6. **Vestibular** – the body's sense of balance
7. **Proprioception** – the body's sense of where it is in space
8. **Interoceptive sens**e – the body's sense of what is going on internally

And to show you how easy it is to stimulate your child's senses, here's a list of fun, simple activities you can try.

Have fun!

EXPLORING

OBSERVATION

COMMUNICATION DEVELOPMENT ATTENTION

IDEAS LISTENING INVESTIGATION

BALANCE

RHYTHM PROBLEM SOLVING

SENSORY MATERIALS CONFIDENCE

CONCENTRATION

MOVEMENT UNDERSTANDING

MAKING FRIENDS SHARING PATIENCE

AWARENESS

SORT AND ORGANISE HAND EYE CO-ORDINATION

CREATIVITY

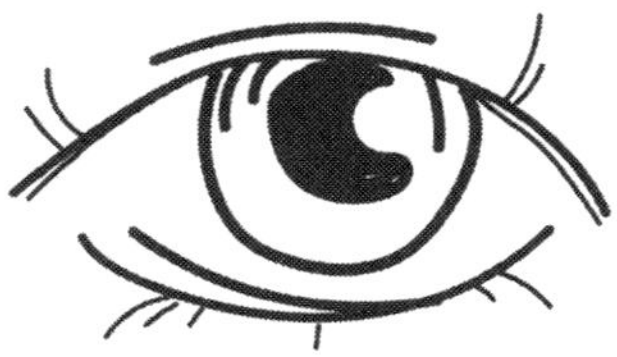

Sight

- Play 'I-spy' and talk about what you see
- Grow sunflowers, pumpkins, or other vegetables
- Look for shapes in the room or when you are out and about
- Draw the outline of what you can see
- Draw with your eyes closed
- Draw on someone's back and see if they can guess what it is
- Make junk art or nature art
- Describe the light intensity
- Take acetates into a bubble bath and make a cylinder of bubbles

Smell

- Smell different herbs and flowers
- Talk about what life would be like if you were a perfume or an aftershave
- Talk about how different foods smell
- Make a sensory garden with scented flowers, bark etc.
- Bake or cook together
- Add different scented oils to modelling dough

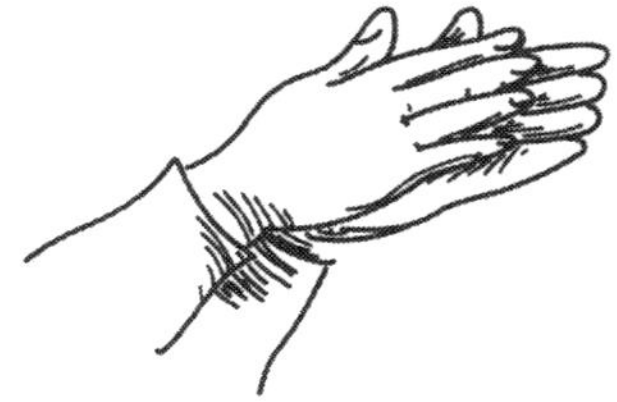

Touch

- Collect shells, stones, mosaics, container lids, or leaves and keep them in a box or basket or create a display with them
- Cover a piece of string with silver foil. On a board, trace the shape with your finger. Try putting different objects under the foil for example a key or a pen
- Describe textures in food, everyday objects, and the things around us
- Create a wiggly trail with a piece of string covered with silver foil and use as a tool to paint with or create patterns
- Cut up a straw and thread onto string or a pipe cleaner to make bracelets, necklaces, or puppets

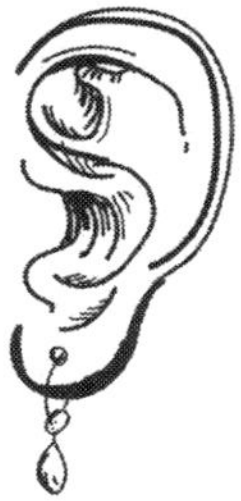

Hearing

- Make sounds with your body such as clapping, stamping, or whistling
- Stop and listen to the sounds around you
- Listen to the sound of running water such as in the bath, at the beach, or by the river
- Try speaking quietly, loudly, fast, and slow
- Talk in a high voice and a low voice
- Make different animal sounds
- Sing

Taste

- Cut different foods into equal sized cubes
- Explore changing the colour of foods using natural food dyes
- Experiment identifying flavours by taking cups of water and adding sugar, salt, lemon, and coffee to taste sweet, salty, sour, and bitter respectively
- Try guessing what certain foods are by tasting blindfolded

Balance

- Be a flamingo and balance on one foot
- Play hopscotch
- Swim
- Skip
- Hop
- Practise forward rolls, handstands, and cartwheels
- Close your eyes and try standing on one leg
- Dance

When you look through this list, how many do you already do?

And that's key... it's likely you've already given your child lots of opportunities to explore their creativity. What's more, when you look through the list of everyday activities above, you can see how simple it can be to make creativity a way of life.

But it's not just the things you do that are important, it's also the way you engage with your children when they are exploring their imagination and creative spark.

Over the years of running The Creation Station activities, we've learnt a lot about the best environment in which to nurture creativity. Here's an overview of The Creation Station approach. I think you'll find it valuable and easy to incorporate some of these principles and approaches into your way of life.

You and your children will benefit too.

Give positive feedback

It sounds obvious doesn't it! But it's SoooOOooo important. Positive feedback and encouragement has a huge impact upon your child. That's because as a parent or carer, you can make your children feel fantastic or awful!

I know, it's not always easy. Sometimes when I'm rushed or stressed I don't tend to listen properly and the effect on my kids is visible. I can see the hurt in their faces. In comparison, when I nurture and support, my kids do great things – just like I did when my mum taught me to believe that I could do anything I put my mind to – they feel more able to just go for it.

Positive feedback is important for another reason...

You see, creativity doesn't have a right or wrong answer. There isn't necessarily a right (or wrong) way to approach a challenge or tackle a problem. But there is your child's way – and nurturing creativity will give your child the opportunity to discover that way.

So be forthcoming with your feedback because your children will instinctively look to you for reassurance and validation. Praise them for their ideas, their imagination, their approach, their thinking, their risk taking – and anything else that you admire in them. In turn you'll boost your child's confidence to trust in their ideas and imagination. This is how creative expression grows. Self-esteem and confidence enables us to explore even deeper into our creative imagination.

Remember to be specific with your feedback too. Avoid generic comments such as "that's great" or "I love that". Instead, be clear about what you valued and admired in particular. This descriptive type of feedback is more useful and meaningful for your child to hear. For example, "I loved how you blended those colours to create that new one." or "That was a really good idea to include buttons in your design. It's given your pictures more texture."

Remember, when it comes to their creative spark, your positive feedback can give your child the confidence to take even more risks with their ideas and imagination. And who knows what amazing places that could lead to.

Let your child lead

If you want your child to find their own voice, you have to let go – even though it's tough. As a grown-up we have more life experience than children. This means we can anticipate 'negative' outcomes. And it's parental instinct to protect our children and keep them away from disappointment.

But do be wary of stepping in to correct or advise. Children (and adults) learn far more if they're able to make a discovery for themselves. That's why creative arts and crafts is more about the journey than the outcome. It's about the discoveries that are made along the way and just sitting back to see what a child will do.

What's more if you correct a child who's being creative, you can begin to sow the seeds that their ideas are wrong or aren't good enough. This in turn stifles their imagination.

I've found that children are far more resourceful than we give them credit for. I remember giving my son a piece of paper and asking him if he could make it fly. I was expecting him to make a paper aeroplane. He didn't. Instead he looked at the paper, rolled it into a ball, and threw it.

It did indeed fly, quite fast in fact – and knocked a cup off the table! I also remember the time I asked the boys how high they could put their hands up? One stretched his arm right up, another stood on his toes, the third stood on a chair.

Make time

Gift children your time. It sounds so easy, but we know the reality is anything but. With multiple pressures it's easy for the day to rush away. And that's why I suggest you start small. For example, my goal is to dedicate just 15 minutes of focused, uninterrupted time with my kids each day. I know it's not loads, but it's an amount I can manage – and it makes a big difference.

During those 15 minutes I do my very best to make my kids know they are the most important person in the world to me. So that means no phone, no tablet, and no distractions. Focus on your child. Make eye contact. Engage with them. Even if you start with just five minutes a day, you'll soon find this time reassures your child how much you truly value them. In turn, this gives your children the confidence to believe in themselves.

Let your child make 'mistakes'

Remember to allow your child to make their own mistakes, if it's safe to do so – and then talk together to work out what happened and what they could do differently next time.

As grown-ups we have more knowledge than children, which makes it tempting to intervene. For example, we know that putting Sellotape onto wet paint means it won't stick. As a result it's tempting to stop your child and tell them not to do it. But when you do, you deny them the chance to discover that information for themselves.

Instead – allow your children to make the 'mistake'. When they put the Sellotape on the wet paint and it doesn't stick, not only have they learned first-hand, but they've experienced problem-solving too – because the likelihood is they'll start to explore a workaround. It's far more empowering.

This is why The Creation Station classes start with an idea – not a project.

We don't set out to make a specific hat, photo frame, or puppet. Creativity isn't about 'here's how you draw a horse'. Our activities are not prescriptive and they are not templated. Instead we start with an idea – and then allow children to get physical with it.

We encourage children to spend time exploring textures, shapes, colours and sounds. You see, the creative process is all about discovery and we aim to inspire children to use their amazing brains and bodies to work things out and create something new.

When we step back, we empower children to make their own learning happen.

Think about when your little one learnt to walk (if indeed they've reached that stage in their development). You'll know they had to learn through trial and error. We learn to walk by falling down. Without the bumps and bruises and occasional tears, from all concerned, we can't learn to develop and grow. We all need positivity and optimism.

Just look at these two scenarios:

"I can't believe you've done it like that" –

can knock confidence

How about:

"That's a really interesting approach you have taken – tell me about it".

When you allow your child to be themselves and nurture and encourage their unique expression, I think you'll find the results are awe-inspiring.

It's a sure-fire way to unlock the wonder within.

Respect the journey - NOT the outcome

School and adult life is very results driven. And whilst it's great to have goals and focus, you can lose sight of the fact that learning is a journey.

Your child doesn't have to achieve a specific outcome for an arts and crafts activity to be a 'success'. They don't need to make something specific to enjoy a worthwhile learning experience.

Instead, it's the journey of discovery and the process of exploration itself that's more valuable.

Take the simple act of painting. Just look at the depth of learning that can take place when a child is allowed to explore simple resources such as paper, paints, and brushes:

- The temperature and texture of the paint, and the way it changes depending on how it's touched
- The way a child can affect their surroundings and change the way the paint looks and moves

- The smell and the different sounds the paint makes as it squelches between their fingers or brush and the funny noises as they apply pressure to the bottle to force the paint out
- The fact that the bottle weighs differently depending on how much paint is in there
- The way some people react differently to them when they have paint on their hands
- The softness of the paint and how it makes their hand slippery and a different colour
- How they can create their own images and marks that are all their own work and that make people smile and say well done!
- The fuzzy feelings inside as they are praised
- How warm water makes their hands feel. How their hands look under water and how paint dissolves and that their hands return to normal and the paint is now somewhere else
- How other children use paint in different ways and how it's OK to be different
- That learning can be fun

As you can see it's not just about putting colour onto paper. It's about all the other 'stuff' that's happening under the radar.

That's the value of the creative process.

Interesting paint fact

Did you know that here at The Creation Station we spend a long time researching and testing products. We are the UK's largest user of Crayola washable paint with over 22,000 litres used each year.

That said it's not easy for us grown-ups to sit back. We like to see a finished product that looks 'good' i.e. how we expect it to look. But you need to let the frustration go if your child doesn't use the 'right colour' or sticks something in the 'wrong place'! Remember, your interference can actually stifle the creative process because you teach your child that their ideas are wrong. What's more, the final creation won't be their own work; it will be influenced by you and not their imagination.

That's why we often say to the parent and carers who come along to our classes, "If you can't scrape your child's creation off the table, don't worry, you've allowed your child to explore and discover freely."

When getting stuck into an activity, instead of teaching and showing – give encouragement, support, and permission to explore and discover.

Encourage concentration

One of the single biggest concerns parents have before their child starts our Little Explorer classes is this:

"My child doesn't sit down for very long so I don't think he/she will enjoy it."

Then after an average of three to five classes, the parents tell us:

"My child sits down longer at The Creation Station than anywhere else!"

Parents, grandparents, and carers are often surprised at how their child's concentration increases throughout our Little Explorer programmes.

There are a number of reasons why this happens:

Firstly, the activities are fun and engaging. From problem-solving to physical projects, to themes that develop a child's emotional intelligence, there's so much going on that a child is often captivated.

The children feel in control and empowered. The Creation Station activities aren't prescriptive. Instead the children are encouraged to use the resources provided to create something that they choose. So because they are playing and creating on their terms, it's more enjoyable.

Finally, the children LOVE having special, quality time with their parent, carer or grandparent. Free from distractions, the adults can get stuck in and fully engage with what their child is doing. Kids thrive on attention and when they get it, they want to continue.

Concentration is a muscle that can be developed. It's a good skill for your child to have (and is essential during adulthood). That's because if they're able to sit tight and focus for extended periods of time, they can get deeper into a problem or create something more complex and intricate – simply because they've had more time to explore and think about the task at hand.

Concentration span does increase with age, but you can influence its development too.

Children who come to our Create Clubs don't come with an adult. Instead they explore with their friends. And just like during Little Explorer sessions, our Creation Station leaders have a whole host of techniques they use to help keep your child (whatever their age) focused and engaged.

Here's a selection of some of the activities that we have developed, tried and tested since 2002. I think they'll help you to extend your child's concentration and focus too.

Bring out the activities gradually

All at once and you'll overwhelm the child, offer too much choice and you'll introduce distractions.

Use a range of painting tools

Variety helps retain interest and stops your child getting distracted too quickly.

Use different parts of the body to paint with

Such as the side of the hand, fingers, knuckles, elbows, and toes. Again, spicing up the activity makes it more interesting and helps keep children focused for longer.

Ask questions

Encourage your child to think about what they're doing. For example:

- Could you use the paintbrush a different way?
- How could you extend this idea?
- Tell me about your creation
- What happens if you put the paint straight on the paper?
- Can you turn the paper round?
- Could you use your other hand?
- Do you want to try and sprinkle different items into the paint – for example, couscous or sea salt? What do you think will happen? (Encourage your child to predict an outcome based on their knowledge).

Extend an activity

Can you transform your picture by adding a collage or texture to it?

- How about making a frame for your picture?
- Can you transform your picture into 3D by gluing or attaching other items?
- Can you make your picture into a mobile or a puppet?
- Can you cut up sections of your painting and stick onto some card to make a greetings card?
- Can you change the speed by which you're drawing/painting? For example, can you paint really s-l-o-w-l-y like you were in space or really fast like a racing car driver?
- What would you do if you were an elephant painting – or a butterfly?

- Can you practice your signature and write your name in lots of different ways?
- Can you fold the piece of paper you're painting in half – or just fold a part of your creation? What happens? How does it change?
- Have a go at creating prints by taking another piece of paper and laying it on top
- Could you lay a shape on top of your painting before you put another piece on top to print? What happens to the negative spaces on the print?
- Can you paint or draw with your eyes closed?
- Try putting a pastel or paint brush between your toes and make some marks
- Can you change a scribble or doodle into a picture
- Would you like to draw something and pass the paper round with a story?
- Try cutting the edges of the paper
- Can you cut up a painting (like a jigsaw) and re-assemble it?
- Why not try scrunched up paper for printing?

And now time for you

What do you want for you and your child?

Take five minutes and write here what you want for your child. As their mummy, daddy, grandparent, or aunty, what do you want for their life?

Then repeat this exercise, but this time think about what you want for you.

Follow the 'Fuzzy Feeling' rules

Finally, let me share our fuzzy feeling factors with you. These are the principles, which make up the framework for The Creation Station experiences. Why don't you try them too?

1

Activities should be fun and not taken too seriously.

2

Allow your child to make mistakes

If you do everything for them they can't learn for them-selves.

3

Don't provide all the answers

Your child will learn far more by doing and working things out for themselves. Let go and allow your little one to develop their thinking and problem-solving skills.

4

Do things together

Spending quality time together is the best way to make your child feel valued and special.

5

Make eye contact with your child and listen when you speak with them.

When you're listening or talking, stop what you are doing, turn around and face them and give them your full attention.

6

Recognise achievements no matter how big or small.

Recognise what your child has done well and tell them specifically what you admire.

7

Smile

It's the most powerful way to convey your feelings.

8

Say,

"Tell me more!"

rather than ask, "What is it?" I promise you'll be amazed what stories your children create. This helps to validate your child's voice and encourages them to share what they think and how they feel.

9 Ask for your child's opinion.

This shows you're interested and value what they think.

10 Give your child opportunities to succeed

Provide opportunities that stretch, but don't pile on the pressure.

11 Let your child know they are loved for who they are.

In this ever-increasing pressurised world, our children need to know they are perfect – just as they are.

12

Say the characteristic you're trying to nurture.

So many children are told they're lazy, naughty, selfish etc., that they soon believe it.

13

Use positive affirmations

Let your child know that you believe in them. Positive words create positive reactions. So, for example, avoid saying, "Don't cross the road." Instead try, "Stay on the kerb close to me." In other words, focus on what you want your child to do.

Part 4

52 tips and creative activities to inspire your child

52 tips & creative activities to inspire your child

Now you've discovered the reasons to nurture your child's creativity, let me share some practical ideas that you can use with your children or children in your care. It's time to put theory into practice – with a little Creation Station inspiration.

The activities described in this section are grouped under the following categories.

1. Communication and language skills
Helping children develop their confidence, speech, and listening skills.

2. Physical development
Helping children develop physical coordination and dexterity with activities that use fine and gross motor skills and by encouraging self-expression or learning through physical activities.

3. Personal, social, and emotional development
Helping children develop a positive sense of themselves, and others; to form positive relationships and develop respect for others; to develop social skills and learn how to manage their feelings; to understand appropriate behaviour in groups; and to have confidence in their own abilities.

4. Mathematical skills
Helping children develop their problem-solving skills so they can analyse, tackle challenges, investigate their ideas and explore issues scientifically.

5. Understanding of their world
Guiding children to make sense of their physical world and their community through opportunities to explore, observe, and find out about people, places, technology, and the environment.

6. Expressive arts and design skills

Enabling children to explore and play with a wide range of media and materials, as well as providing opportunities and encouragement for sharing their thoughts, ideas and feelings through a variety of activities in art, music, movement, dance, role play, and design and technology.

7. Activities that encourage children to enjoy a variety of food

To help avoid fussiness with food and encourage children to feel comfortable experimenting with different tastes, textures, and flavours.

8. Activities to play together

To help build strong family bonds and encourage families to explore, play, and create as a unit.

9. Easy, low-cost activity ideas to inspire your child on a rainy day

Because you can never have enough suggestions to keep active, curious children, occupied on those days when you can't get outside.

As well as nurturing your child's creativity, all these activities are designed to support their learning and development too. That's because these activities are underpinned by the Early Years Foundation Stages (EYFS). These are statutory framework for early years that sets the standards for learning, development and care for children from birth to five in England (23). We have created extension activities so that older children can benefit too.

We've spent over sixteen years developing our programmes and even now we tweak and change in light of developments. On the following pages, I'll share with you some of the most powerful and positive ideas and activities we've tried – so you can inspire your child.

Are you ready for the creative journey to begin?

Then let's get stuck in!

Creative activities that nurture communication and language skills

You can nurture your child's communication and language skills through the following activities:

- Speaking
- Storytelling
- Retelling
- Debating
- Presenting
- Reading aloud
- Dramatising
- Book making
- Researching
- Listening
- Writing

The ability to communicate so our thoughts and contributions can be heard is one of life's most essential skills. Our instinct to communicate starts from the moment we're born and our skills develop and evolve, as we get older.

It's important that children learn to communicate in both verbal and in non-verbal ways. And one of the best ways that you can help your child communicate their thoughts, feelings, concerns and ideas, is through active listening.

There is a very moving, still face experiment, carried out by Dr Edward Tronick in 1978. (24) It shows the hugely negative impact upon a baby not receiving the acknowledgment they need.

I remember the first time Sam watched TV. The presenter was saying hello and chatting, Sam said hello back, and got no response. So he tried again. After three times, he just sat still. We quickly learn when a person isn't interested in communicating with us.

As you explore these activities (and through your day-to-day life), I highly recommend taking the time to stop what you are doing and turn and look at your child when they're communicating with you.

When you value your child, and acknowledge that they have a contribution to make, it makes them feel recognised, and seen, which in turn boosts their self-esteem – both of which are important for future mental health and overall well-being.

There are lots of activities you can do to enhance communication skills. Here is just a couple to get you started.

Idea 1

Create a story

Explore this activity to help your child develop their interest in stories and reading while enhancing their conversation, imagination, and thinking skills.

First choose a book that you'd like to explore with your child. Next find various props that will help your child tell the story. You can use anything from puppets or props to cards. You could even use your child's own drawings.

Time needed 30min +

Items needed: A book, toys, cards, maps and puppets.

Adapt for younger children:
Read the book out loud to your child and bring out a relevant prop as the story progresses. For example, if you were reading the Hungry Caterpillar, you could introduce different food items. When you've finished the story, consolidate with a relevant arts and crafts activity.

As you extend your story telling experiences, remember to add to your prop collection. Familiarity with items provides a strong sense of value and recognition for your child.

Adapt for older children:
Instead of reading the book out loud, introduce a prop and encourage your child to tell the story to you. As your child grows in confidence, you could encourage them to choose an appropriate prop. Not only does this approach encourage your child's imagination, it also helps their story telling too.

Remember this doesn't have to be serious. This is a fun way to encourage your child to talk through stories. If your child's imagination takes over, go with it.

NDEBELE

Story Maker

As well as reading a story from a book, use a story bag to inspire children to make up their own tale.

Choose a range of age-appropriate props and place them into a story bag. Next, encourage your child to select one prompt at a time and talk about it to create a story from scratch.

Remember to use open-ended questions to pull out additional thoughts and extend the story. This approach will help develop your child's vocabulary and language skills too. Ask questions such as, "What happens next?" "Tell me more." or "How did that happen?" You can also use this activity with a number of children and encourage them to take turns to develop the story.

You'll find each story maker session will be different – and I'm sure you'll enjoy lots of giggles as each unique story takes its own funny turns and twists.

Time needed 30min +

Items needed: Book, bag, toys, cards, puppets and household items.

Adapt for younger children:
Fill the story bag with objects such as a wooden spoon, woolly hat, flip-flop, teddy etc. Then take turns to choose an object and continue the story. Alternatively, put animal toys or pictures into the bag and as they are picked out ask your child to make a noise and move around the room like the animal they've chosen.

Adapt for older children:
Encourage your child to make cards containing words or pictures for the story maker bag. You can use photos, draw your own, or cut pictures and words out of magazines (or use a mixture of all three). Everyone takes a turn to pick a card and then use that word/picture to develop the story.

Creative activities that nurture physical development

You can nurture your child's physical development through the following activities:

- Hands-on learning
- Physical activities
- Changing room arrangements
- Creative movement
- Field trips, excursions, and adventures
- Crafts
- Drama
- Researching
- Groups
- Dancing

You may be familiar with recent studies and news reports that highlight the potentially negative effects that tablets and touchscreen devices can have on a child's physical development. For example, swiping screens may reduce children's ability to gauge pressure and build strength in their fingers and hands.

This is not to say that use of technology is negative for children. Quite the opposite... We live in a world where technological advances are happening at a phenomenal rate where cutting-edge creative thinking is taking us to places we never imagined a decade ago. But like all things, a balanced and varied range of activities will provide a much more rounded and grounded experience.

The following fun activities can be used alongside modern tech to help your child develop these important physical skills.

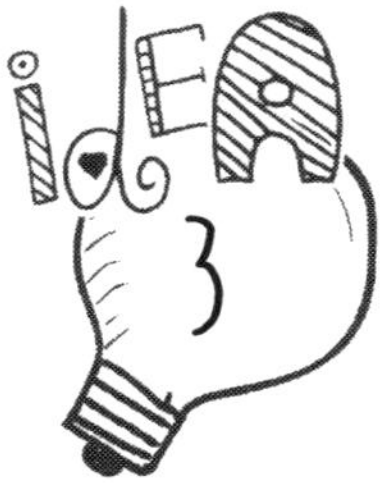

Make your own instruments

Playing musical instruments can inspire your child to become more body confident as well as helping them develop movement, rhythm, and fine motor skills. Of course, music makes you feel good too!

Using items that are lying around the house, encourage your child to make a range of home-made musical instruments. For example, you can create a drum set using empty food tins or saucepans, lids, and spoons for drumsticks. You can turn a cereal box into a shaker and you can blow across the tops of straws or bottles to create flute like tunes. Then, with instruments in hand, encourage your child to dance, jiggle, wiggle and giggle.

Time needed

1hr +

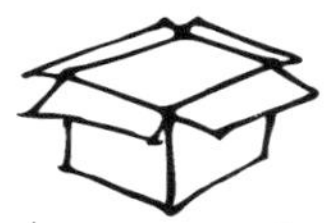

Items needed

Empty clean food tins, balloons, straws, empty boxes, dry food items, elastic and masking tape.

Adapt for younger children:
Younger children LOVE making their own musical shakers. Give your child a plastic cup (see-through ones work well as you can see what's inside) and invite them to fill it with their favourite ingredients. Rice, pasta, and other dried beans and pulses make brilliant noises! Seal the lid with sticky tape or a lid and you're finished. You can extend this activity by encouraging your child to decorate their shaker with stickers. You can even attach long strings of crepe paper to create a flowing effect.

Adapt for older children:
Transform the shaker into a person with a face, arms, and wiggly legs so they move when they shake. Feel free to name Mr or Mrs Shaker too.

be a ....

Idea 4

Hand and footprint art

Understanding their body and its capabilities is key to a child's physical development. That's why hands and feet are such brilliant artwork tools!

Encourage your child to explore the marks they can make with their hands and feet. Simply provide big sheets of paper and plenty of paint and see what happens.

Adapt for younger children:
Many young children have no problem painting their own bodies. For some of the messier activities you may find it easier to pop the children in the bath with no water and the heating turned up. Here are a few ideas to enjoy:

- Draw around your child's hands and feet and let them do the same to you. Then use your drawings to talk about different sizes and identify different parts.
- Finger, hand, and foot painting are always firm favourites! To get a print, either press the paper onto your child's hand/or hold your child and gently lower them towards the paper. You'll find they'll instinctively open their hand as they come nearer to the floor.
- Play rhyme games such as 'round and round the garden' or 'this little piggy'.
- Then when your hands and feet are clean, use some moisturising cream to finish the activity with a hand or foot massage.

Adapt for older children:
Let your child make their own prints. Once dry, encourage them to turn the prints into something else. For example, can they make their name with handprints?

Alternatively, try creating a 3D hand or foot by creating curves to represent your fingers/toes. A ballpoint pen is a great tool for this type of more detailed activity.

Items needed: Wallpaper or lining paper, paint, bare hands and feet.

Time needed: 45min +

idEA 5

Reach & stretch

By encouraging your child to use their whole body when creating, you'll inspire them to appreciate their physicality and develop their self-confidence.

Roll out a long piece of wallpaper or tape two pieces of plain lining paper side by side. Then use this blank canvas to inspire your child to experiment with different marks and patterns. For example:

- You could sketch out a word, which they can colour in
- They could mark how far they can stretch with different colours, pens, crayons, paints, and pens
- Experiment with different paint applicators such as decorating rollers or big brushes
- Have a go at drawing around each other, a toy, or each other to create 'Big Art' and then cut out when dry
- Draw a life-sized outline of a person and turn it into a superhero, a sportsperson (or anything else that inspires your child)

Adapt for younger children:
Give your child a range of tools and encourage them to practice their finger movements over a large canvas. This will help develop their hand-eye coordination.

Adapt for older children:
Encourage them to create a favourite landscape and use different tools and materials to collage the image.

Items needed

Wallpaper or lining paper,
paint, crayons, pens and pencils.

Time needed

30min +

Idea 6

Fingerprint art and portraits

This activity is great for improving dexterity and focusing in on the detail. This activity not only uses your child's imagination but also provides an extension idea for children who love painting with their body.

This activity can be done individually or with friends. Pop fingers into paint or press onto an ink pad and then blot to remove any residue. With the paint applied your child can go wild and make patterns with their fingerprints on a blank canvas of their choice.

Time needed: 45min +

Items needed: Paper or canvas, paint or ink pads, wet flannel and felt pens.

Adapt for younger children:
Try using this activity to encourage younger children to explore and experiment with different colours. As an extension, you can ask open questions to encourage children to notice how different fingers make prints of different sizes.

Adapt for older children:
Supply felt pens or fine point pens and transform each print into something else. For example, you could create portraits, animals, vehicles – whatever your imagination can conjure up.

We've taken fingerprint portraits to lots of schools where children have created everything from a class picture to a gift for a retiring headteacher. You can use the same idea at home too. For example, for my mum's 80th birthday we created a family portrait based on our fingerprints where everyone added their own mark.

Make a salt dough model

Making salt dough models is a brilliant way to help children develop their dexterity, finger movements, and thinking.

Make your own salt dough and then mould into shapes of your choice. Simply mix together the ingredients and get making. You can even make different coloured doughs by adding some paint and allowing your child to squish the mixture and watch the transformation.

Remember, you can 'cook' a finished salt dough creation in the oven at a low temperature. You can tell when the item is 'baked' because it goes very hard (a bit like my cakes!) You can then make the model shiny by applying PVA glue or paint.

Adapt for younger children:
Introduce the modelling material and encourage your child to explore its texture and temperature. Help them to discover how it's easier to manipulate and change the dough when the material is warm and has been in their hands for longer.

You can experiment with different shape cutters or tools like a pizza cutter. Alternatively, roll the dough into a sausage shape to make a basket or a snake. You could even find some objects to stick into the dough to create different effects. Usually children don't need much direction. Just give them the opportunity and let them experiment with shapes and texture.

Adapt for older children:
You can stretch older children's modelling skills by giving them different types of clay, so they can explore the different textures and the different results. For example, as well as salt dough offer Play-Doh, silk clay, or foam clay.

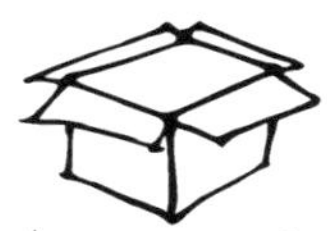

Items needed

A cup of salt, a cup of flour, water, PVA glue (if planning to 'bake') and paint.

Time needed

30min +

Clay is very popular with older children and it's a resource we use frequently in our workshops. Children love creating objects such as funky pencil toppers and alien creatures. Alternatively, your child could craft something out of clay which they later attach to a key ring, wooden frame, canvas, card, or magnet. (Remember magnets are very dangerous if swallowed. So please ensure children are supervised when using them).

In addition to traditional clay, foam and silk clay are brilliant materials to explore and work with. They have a great texture and are easy to manipulate and cause very little mess. They even become bouncy after they've been left to dry for a couple of days. In fact, these items are among the top sellers in our online craft shop.

Play-Doh

Play-Doh also remains a popular favourite. We were delighted when Hasbro approached us to develop and deliver Play-Doh themed classes and events across the country. We loved supporting over 75,000 children and families with hands-on, tactile Play-Doh themed experiences.

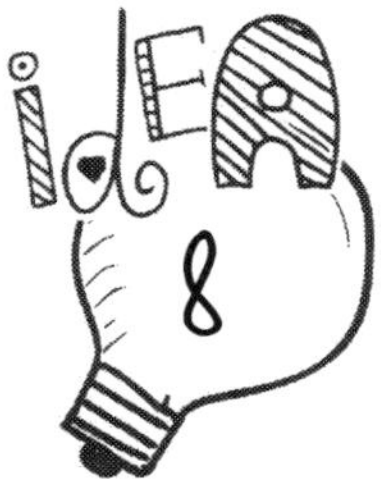

Hug & tickle

Encourage physical development, laughter, and plenty of family fun with these super simple physical contact games.

Physical contact is an important way to nurture your child's physical development. Everything from hugs, bouncing, carrying, piggybacks, wrestle tickling, wheelbarrow races, and ball games all offer learning opportunities as well as plenty of fun and family bonding.

Adapt for younger children:
Use nursery rhymes to build up to a tickle!

Adapt for older children:
Create an obstacle course in the house or set up races in the garden that involve going through a tickle machine.

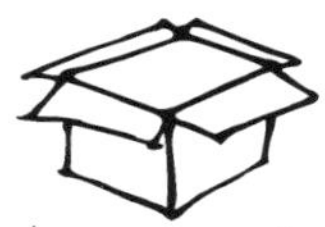

Items needed

Friends and family to play with.

Time needed

15min +

Activities to nurture your child's personal, social, and emotional development

You can nurture your child's personal, social, and emotional development with the following activities:

- Social contact
- Parties
- Learning with others
- Sharing
- Group work
- Being part of a club
- Peer teaching
- Social awareness
- Conflict mediation
- Discussing
- Mixing with different ages
- Brainstorming together

It's important we provide children with the skills they need to become actively involved in the world around them.

- Personal development is a skill that helps children to understand who they are and what they can do
- Social development explores how children come to understand themselves in relation to others. This includes making friends, understanding the rules of society, and behaviour towards others
- Emotional development concerns the way children understand their own and others' feelings. It's about empathy and being able to see a situation from someone else's perspective

Together, these three areas provide a solid foundation that can help children build relationships, manage feelings and behaviour, and develop self-confidence and self-awareness.

Armed with these skills, children can go through life knowing how to get on with others while developing the confidence they need to be true to themselves. The following activities can help.

Active listening

Listening to hear, not to speak helps your child feel valued and boosts their self-esteem.

We all know people who, when you speak with them, are just waiting for their chance to take the floor. They aren't really listening and don't fully hear what you have to say. In comparison, active listening is about not changing the topic of conversation to a subject that suits you. Instead, it's about listening to fully understand. Therefore, active learning is a great communication skill for children to develop because it will help them develop empathy and build stronger relationships with the people they care about.

Here are two brilliant activities to help older children develop their listening skills.

What would you do?

Read or make up a story that describes different situations between two friends. Then use the story as a platform to discuss choices and possible outcomes with your child. You can ask questions such as:

- How do you think the characters felt?
- What would you do in that situation?
- Why would you do that?
- How might the characters handle things differently?

For extra fun, why not act it out.

Person of interest

Another great listening game is to interview someone. Start by asking your child what interests them and what they would like to discover more about. For example, do they want to learn more about tractors, their grandfather's childhood, or a particular job? Once your child has chosen their person of interest, help them to write down their questions and then organise the interview.

Adapt for younger children:
Encourage your child to interview some of their toys. Your child can talk for the toys and create a whole new world and characters for their toys.

Adapt for older children:
Encourage your child to record the interview (with permission) and then write down the answers. They can extend this activity by crafting a story or creating some art.

Items needed — Pens, paper and someone to interview.

Time needed — 1hr

Idea 10

Body language charades

We communicate far more through our bodies than we do through our words. This alternative game of charades is an excellent way to show your child how much their body actually talks and reveals.

Body language charades encourages children to develop their emotional intelligence while helping them to understand how others feel based on the expressions they make.

- Brainstorm different emotions and write each on a separate piece of card
- Put the cards into a bag or a hat
- Take turns to choose a card
- Act out the emotion so the others can guess

You can emphasise facial expressions and use body language to help communicate, but you're not allowed to make any sounds!

Time needed: 15min +

Items needed: Cards with emotions listed, a hat or a bag.

Adapt for younger children:
Extend this activity by encouraging your child to explore different actions with different emotions. They might associate happiness with skipping, or anger with someone running. The goal here is to help children understand why people may do certain things when they feel a particular way.

Adapt for older children:
Talk about all the different types of behaviours there are and ask them for some examples of when they have felt like this or have seen other people show these feelings.

IDEA 11

Empathy investigators

Empathy is a crucial social skill. It will help your child interact more effectively with others if they have an awareness of what the people around them think and feel.

Show your child pictures of people or characters. Ask your child the following questions and discuss their responses:

- What do you think this person is feeling?
- What do you notice about how they're standing or sitting?
- What does their body language say?

You can do this activity whilst reading a story, watching a show, or people watching when you're out and about.

You can also adapt and extend this activity by asking your child why they think a character, or a person has made a particular choice. For example, ask them what motivates Pooh Bear to find the honey or why the family try to run away from the bear during their bear hunt. Talking about what motivates people to behave in a certain way helps children to gain a better understanding of their behaviour – as well as building their awareness of the actions of the people they meet.

Time needed: 30min +

Items needed: People to watch – in person, books, movies or cartoons

Adapt for younger children:
Keep your questions simple. When they respond, recognise their contribution. If they haven't got it right, rather than saying that's wrong, thank them for their idea. You could use words such as that is really close, or yes it could be that and it could also be...?

Adapt for older children:
Ask them to share examples with you and talk about them together. My sister, Fran plays a game with my boys when they are out and about or people watching. They guess what jobs people do, for example, undercover spies, astronauts, or alien zappers!

IDEA 12

Interview your feelings

Emotional intelligence is about understanding why people feel and behave differently in different circumstances. Often, children react with strong emotions because they don't know how to articulate their feelings. As emotional intelligence develops, children can deal better with the situations and social settings they face.

We've all been there. Your child has a meltdown in the most unfortunate of places and there's nothing you can do to calm them down. It can be challenging when your child is angry, and we can often respond the same way. But it's helpful to remember we are the adults! So instead of getting angry, try to show understanding and give a name to the feeling. For example, "It sounds like you are feeling really angry about not being able to have the xxx? I can understand why you might be feeling like this."

This approach helps your child to recognise there are lots of different emotions. You don't have to agree with how they feel, but acknowledging your child's response can help them feel understood, listened to, and valued. Do be aware that your facial expressions and body language need to match the words you are saying and the tone you are using.

Adapt for younger children:
Try drawing different circles with different faces in to show that you are OK with being able to express how you feel.

Adapt for older children:
Once things have calmed down after an emotional occasion, try to make time to talk about how your child felt. This isn't about judging their reactions, but allowing them to express themselves openly. You'll find this strategy will help them open up and talk to you more as they grow older.

Items needed

Something to write and draw on, paints, crayons, pens and pencils.

Time needed

15min +

Idea 13

Scrapbooking

Scrapbooking encourages your child to talk and think about what they've been doing. Through pictures, journaling, drawing, collages, stickers and more, you can help bring your child's reflective process to life.

The great thing about this activity is it's entirely personal, as every child can use their scrapbook in the way that best expresses their interests and memories. Provide children with a big paper book and encourage them to capture memories and mementos. We recently introduced reflective scrapbooking into Creation Station classes. Every week children work on their 'Exploration Journal'. As well as creating a keepsake, the journal has become a valuable journal that's helped parents and children talk about and share what they've done.

Time needed 1hr +

Items needed A scrapbook, glue, sticky tape, pens, pencils and crayons.

Adapt for younger children:
This activity creates a great way to talk about things you've done together. Remember to ask your child questions such as: Do you remember when we... what did you think of... tell me how you felt when we did... etc.

Adapt for older children:
Encourage your child to keep their own scrapbook of things they come across that they like. This can include anything from tickets to places they've been, reminders of things they'd like to do, or even wrappers or stickers from their favourite sweets or foods.

IdEA 14

Build a fort or den

Encouraging children to build their own hideaway with household or garden items is a brilliant way to nurture teamwork and creativity.

Not only is fort building brilliant for developing team-building skills, but once built, your child will have a unique base for imaginative play.

Den building is a fun opportunity to practice creativity and communication. Children are able to look at everyday objects through different eyes and figure out how they can piece them together to create a hideaway. You can supervise, give suggestions, and make sure everyone is being safe, but don't help too much! There's a lot of benefit in your child learning to work with siblings or friends towards a common goal.

Time needed: 1hr 30min +

Items needed: Pillows, blankets, cushions, duvet and a cardboard box.

Adapt for younger children:
Try pulling out a couch or place a long tablecloth over a table. Alternatively, help them create a little cardboard box den for their toys. If an empty box captures their imagination, you could provide some brushes or paint, so they can decorate their den. You could even cut a doorway flap so they can crawl in and out.

Adapt for older children:
The world really is your oyster. You could create your own design together or encourage them to create their own. Let them have fun and dream big! For example, build a race car, rocket, castle, house, or space machine. And once the den is built, extend the activity with a picnic and some stories.

Creative activities that nurture your child's mathematical skills

You can nurture your child's mathematical development with the following activities:

- Problem-solving
- Measuring, sequencing
- Thinking
- Predicting
- Playing logic games
- Collecting data
- Experimenting
- Solving puzzles
- Classifying
- Using tools
- Discovering what happens when
- Using money
- Comparing and contrasting information

People often overlook the huge benefits that creativity can bring to maths and science.

It's one of the reasons why some schools are exploring a creative arts approach to the STEM subjects of science, technology, engineering, and maths.

When you look at the working practices of many of the great inventors and entrepreneurs, you'll find that they thought out of the box. They tried many different approaches and were able to persevere even when many doubted them.

With my own boys, their maths teachers have all commented on how they work with problems in a very creative way. Often, they will think around the whole problem to find solutions.

Many schools are incorporating arts into the STEM subject creating the acronym STEAM (where the additional A stands for art). This has the intention of nurturing students' curiosity and helping them develop creativity, problem-solving, and critical thinking skills.

Here are some activities that can help develop these important skills.

Go on a texture hunt

This activity allows your child to explore different shapes, textures, and colours so they can develop sensory and observation skills as well as their understanding of the world around them.

Give your child a bag, a box, or a tray and then challenge them to look around the home and find items that fit a particular category. For example, you could ask them to find objects that are shiny, bumpy, or rough. Alternatively, you could invite them to make a collection of red objects or to find objects that are round.

If you run out of ideas simple ask your child to set the next challenge!

Time needed 45min +

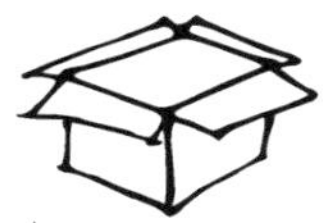

Items needed

A bag, tray or box to collect items, a location of your choice.

Adapt for younger children:
You can use this activity to develop your child's recognition skills by inviting them to find specific objects such as:

- Something that's a particular shape such as round or square
- Their favourite things
- A particular colour
- Something healthy to eat
- A collection of items that are all the same colour

Adapt for older children:
Try setting a specific time limit and encourage older children to look more thoroughly to find more objects. Then, as an extension when they've completed their collection, you could invite them to use their findings to inspire some artwork. They could create some art with their collection. They could collage or draw around the objects they've found, or even paint with them. This is a great open-ended activity that can stimulate growing minds to think laterally.

Go on a tiny adventure

Use this activity to encourage your child to see the smaller things they may not have observed before. This activity is a simple, but effective way to develop their sense of scale and proportion

This activity can be done inside on a rainy day or outside if you're exploring the beach, your local woodlands or the park. Give your child a small box (such as an empty tea bag box or a jewellery box) and challenge them to see how many objects they can fit inside. Once their collection is finished, you can explore the contents of the box together and extend the activity. For example, you could count the items, sort them by shape, size, and colour, or even discuss where they might have come from and what each item could be used for.

Time needed 45min +

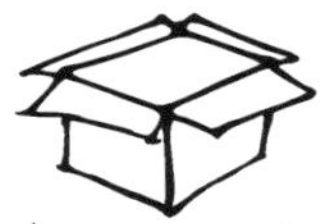

Items needed: A box, a location (indoors or outdoors), glue, sticky tape, cardboard, colouring pens, pencils and crayons.

Adapt for younger children:
Once your child had returned from their tiny adventure, create a collage with the items found by gluing them onto a piece of card.

Adapt for older children:
Encourage your child to create a picture by drawing around each of their items. The items could be laid out separately on a piece of paper or drawn to overlap each other. Finally, colour in the shapes to create a tiny masterpiece.

IDEA 17

Pouring with dried food

This activity helps children explore how solids and liquids move differently. Pouring is also a brilliant way to discover different mediums by comparing and contrasting them.

Depending on the age of your child, take a tray and a number of different sized cups and bowls. Explore different dry ingredients such as pasta or couscous and encourage your child to pour from one cup into another.

Time needed 30min +

Items needed Containers of various sizes, dried pasta, pulses, rice and a tray.

Adapt for younger children:
As your child pours, ask extension questions to help them explore the objects they're playing with. For example, you can ask them which objects are bigger, smaller, heavier, or lighter. You can also encourage sensory play by encouraging your child to feel the different textures and listen to the various sounds the dried food makes. And as you're unlikely to want to eat poured items after the game has finished, why not extend this activity by sticking the dried food onto a piece of card.

Adapt for older children:
Include a set of scales and encourage your child to weigh out different amounts and even calculate the difference. As an extension, you could explore weighing feathers, tissues, stones and other objects. Weave in estimation by asking your child what they think different objects might weigh and then talk about why different items are different weights.

Household games

Clearing away and washing up can be made fun. What's more, including these activities from a young age helps children understand there are consequences to their actions – if you take something out it will stay there until you put it away.

Children who join in with the washing up and tidying away develop a range of useful skills and experiences. For example, they learn to organise items and put them away in the right place (so they can find them again). They learn how to look after belongings and they also learn about consequences. For example, when food is put on plates they need to be washed before they can be used again.

And if that's not enough, involving your child in daily tasks is a great way to spend time with them. As children grow older they can join in more tasks – anything from clearing up to washing up and food prep.

Adapt for younger children:
A washing-up bowl with bubbles can provide a wealth of pouring and fun activities. If you have access to an outdoor tap and hose you can encourage younger children to have a go at scrubbing the patio or cleaning the car. Alternatively, to minimise spillages, take a washing-up bowl outside and allow your child to get busy. Pop them in a splash suit and let them wash some plastic crockery, toys, and other objects that won't get damaged by water.

We couldn't find the perfect splashsuit so we designed our own for our baby and preschool Creation Station classes. We even won a Creative Play award for our all-in-one splashsuits. Due to popular demand we now sell them in the craft shop section of our website.

Adapt for older children:
If your child is old enough, let them help you by standing at the sink or on a chair at the sink. Make sure you stay close at hand to keep your little one safe and stable.

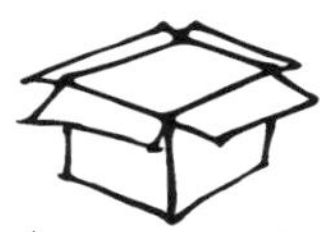

Items needed

Everyday household chores and patience!

(Children often take longer than us adults!)

Time needed

30min +

Activities that nurture your child's understanding of their world

You can nurture your child's understanding of the world with the following activities:

- Being involved in everyday activities with you
- Reading outside
- Cloud watching
- Identifying insects
- Building habitats
- Identifying plants
- Using a magnifying glass
- Going on a nature walk
- Building a garden
- Studying the stars
- Bird watching
- Collecting rocks
- Making bird feeders
- Going to trips to the zoo or garden centre
- Even watching a tumble dryer!

Creative activities provide first-hand experiences (in a safe and nurturing environment) that allow children to explore, discover, and learn 'what if...?'

There are many things that we, as adults, take for granted that children need to learn. That's why fun experiments with frozen ice cubes or cloud and star gazing can be so valuable. When you allow children to discover something for themselves, that knowledge is more likely to stick. Children also get the sense of satisfaction that they figured it out. It helps instil a sense of pride and self-responsibility. In addition, creative experiments and activities (such as those contained in this section), help children develop their creative intelligence because they have the space and opportunities to test, develop, and stretch their understanding.

Without creative intelligence our children are less prepared for the challenges that life and society bring. It's creative intelligence that empowers our imagination to visualise something unique or create alternatives. Creativity is all about making new connections, which spark the unexpected and enable new possibilities.

The activities in this section all deepen a child's understanding of their world, as well as encourage them to unleash their imagination and the wonder within.

idea 19

Sensory walks and leaf printing

Collecting and talking about natural treasures while exploring the great outdoors is an easy, inexpensive way to discover the wonders around us. It's a perfect excuse to nurture sensory skills too.

Pull on the wellies or some sturdy shoes and go on a nature trail to collect some leaves for painting. Use the nature walk to encourage your child to use their senses and observe the wide range of plants and structure surrounding them. Do explain that not all plants are good to touch or eat.

- Invite your child to take notice of the leaf's shape and colour. Ask them to spot the difference between the different sides
- Discuss how leaves change according to the seasons and why
- Ask them to describe how different leaves feel and smell
- If you find edible leaves (such as mint) you can ask your child to describe the taste – but take time to explain why they can't taste all leaves
- And if it's autumn, remember to explore the sound dry leaves make by making a pile and jumping in it!

Back at home you can get busy with leaf painting. Simply brush some paint onto a leaf and press onto paper to make different patterns. You can either make one big picture or cut out individual leaves and peg them up on a makeshift string washing line.

Adapt for younger children:
While painting, talk about the different shapes, colours, sizes and textures and explore which side of the leaf makes the best print.

Adapt for older children:
Experiment with turning leaf prints into leaf creatures. Simply take some googly eyes, a hole punch, and some pipe cleaners and get creative. Ask your child what ideas they have.

Items needed

Wallpaper or lining paper, brushes, paints, googly eyes, sequins and glue.

Time needed

1hr 30min +

Idea 20

Create a bug hotel

By observing mini beasts, your child can develop respect and understanding of the natural world. It's an activity that also allows them to see life from a totally different perspective.

This quick and easy activity is a great way to explore and discover more about the little creatures that live in our gardens and parks. All you need is a handful of straws, a plastic cup, some string, and scissors.

Simply cut the straws to a length that makes them flush with the top of a cup. Then pack the straws tightly into the cup to create a cosy bug hotel. Finally place the bug house behind a rock and then revisit a few days later to see if anything has moved in.

Time needed: 30min +

Items needed: Plastic cups, straws and scissors.

Adapt for younger children:
Go exploring in the garden or park and move some stones to show the number of little creatures that live hidden away. See if you can count all the bugs and beasties that you see. Do remember to wash your hands afterwards.

Adapt for older children:
Encourage your child to make a model of a bug. If they aren't keen on the bugs, talk about other insects like a butterfly instead.

For bugs, take some clay, pipe cleaners, and googly eyes. For butterflies, fold paper in a concertina fashion around a pipe cleaner. Finally, attach a length of string so they can flutter in the wind.

Idea 21

Make ice balls

This is a simple yet fun activity that allows your child to develop their understanding of temperature and how things change state.

When my three boys, Sam, Ollie, and Josh were small we had great fun making ice balls to play with. It's such an easy activity too. Simply fill a balloon with water until it's the size of a grapefruit. Then tie the balloon and place into the freezer. You can add a few drops of food colouring or paint to create patterns in the ice balls.

After a few days, remove the balloon and put it into the bath at bath time. You can then encourage your child to explore how it responds to the warm water. For example, does it float? What happens as you peel away the outer plastic? How does the ice feel contrasted against the warm bath? How does the ice change in time? You can also use these balls in the garden, but do be careful, as they are very hard when thrown! (Yes I do speak from experience!)

Time needed: 20min +

Items needed: Balloons, water and a freezer.

Adapt for younger children:
Add some warm water and washing-up liquid to a washing-up bowl. Agitate the water to create lots and lots of bubbles. Encourage your child to scoop up the bubbles and blow them. If it's a warm day you'll notice that they float in the air! Then scoop some of the bubbles into a container and pop them in the freezer for 24 hours. Once frozen let your child discover crunchy bubbles. Chat through why they think that they have changed.

Adapt for older children:
Another variation on this activity is the Ice Freeze, which also encourages children to explore the effect of freezing items. For example, pop toys into a cup of water. You could explore the different effects of adding food colouring or paint into the water before you freeze it. And don't forget the defrost. Simply take the frozen objects out into the garden and see how long the toys take to 'hatch'.

Idea 22

Speedy seedy bird cake

Spending time in the outdoors is a good way to encourage children to respect the natural world and develop their understanding of how other creatures live and survive in the wild.

You can encourage visitors to your garden by providing food. This Speedy Seedy Bird Cake, shared here with kind permission of the RSPB (25), is easy and fun to make with little ones. Remember to wash your hands before and after this activity and please note this isn't for human consumption – even if it does look very tasty, and is not suitable to make if you have nut allergies!

Time needed 1hr 30min +

Items needed: Bird seed, raisins, peanuts, cheese, lard or suet, yoghurt pots, string, a mixing bowl and scissors.

Adapt for younger children:
Make a hole in the bottom of a yoghurt pot and thread through a long piece of string. Then tie a knot inside the yoghurt pot so the pot can hang upside down. Let the lard warm to room temperature and then mix all the food ingredients in a bowl. Squidge everything together and fill the yoghurt pots. Pop in the fridge to set for an hour or so. Hang up in your garden and then watch the visiting birds enjoy their feast.

Adapt for older children:
Encourage older children to look online or in a bird book to identify their garden visitors. Invite your child to draw the birds they see. They could even create their own wildlife book or a journal that tracks and records visitors.

Idea 23

Make a beaded, bug note hanger

Using and transforming everyday objects can be great fun and low cost. It also encourages children to think laterally and helps them see everyday objects through fresh, imaginative eyes.

Paint one side of a clothes peg and stick double-sided tape to the other. Cut out some card handprints and attach to the double-sided tape. Next, poke pipe cleaners through the middle of the peg and thread with beads. Bend the beaded pipe cleaners to create loops to make wings and twist the ends of the pipe cleaners to make the antenna.

Finish by popping a piece of ribbon through the middle of the peg so your child can hang up their masterpiece. Once finished, your beaded peg can be used to hold anything from the weekly shopping list to a photograph.

Encourage your child to keep their own recycling box filled with interesting items and objects that can be transformed.

Time needed 45min +

Items needed: A clothes peg, double-sided tape, pipe cleaners, beads, card and paint.

Adapt for younger children:
Threading is great for developing hand-eye coordination so experiment with pipe cleaners, beads and buttons to help your child develop this important skill.

Adapt for older children:
There are lots of creative ways to approach this activity. For example, older children could use the peg to create characters that have a long mouth such as crocodiles, snappy fish, or bugs covered with pom poms. Simply provide some materials and see what peg creation your child invents.

Press leaves

Autumn is a great time to study the changing colour of leaves. This simple activity combines outdoor exploring with an at-home extension activity.

On a windy day, go for a walk and try to catch a leaf, it's not as easy as it sounds. After plenty of leaf kicking and scrunching, help your child collect some dry leaves. Take them home and place them between two books to press. After a few days, take the leaves out and discover how they've changed.

Time needed: 30min +

Items needed: Leaves, paper, glue, paints, felt pens and heavy books.

Adapt for younger children:
Give your child some sheets of paper and glue so they can create some leaf inspired artwork. Use paints, crayons, or felt pens too so they can add their own artistic touch to the leafy creation.

Adapt for older children:
Encourage your child to use their imagination to invent different ways to use their leaves. For example, they could create beautiful bookmarks, a collage, or a mobile.

Make a twig friend

This simple activity helps your child develop their decision-making and thinking skills as well as exploring how different materials can work together to create something new.

Explore on a woodland walk and collect sticks along the way. Then, at home decorate the stick and transform it into a twig friend.

When doing this activity ask your child to give their twig a name. Ask them to tell you more about their friend. Next, encourage your child to explore different materials to decorate their friend. For example, you could paint the twigs, use string or ribbon to bind sticks together, glue on fabric, or add pipe cleaner arms and googly eyes. By exploring a range of materials your child will be able to discover their favourites and what they feel works best for their twig friend.

Adapt for younger children:
Once the twig friends are complete, create a little story together about twigs.

Adapt for older children:
Encourage your child to develop a puppet show featuring their twig friends. Alternatively, invite your child to create a home for their twig friends.

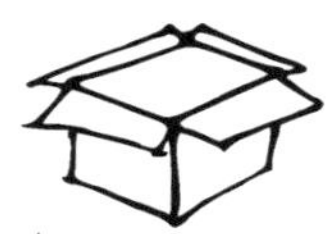

Items needed

Twigs, glue, paints, fabrics, string, googly eyes and pipe cleaners.

Time needed

45min +

Activities that nurture your child's expressive arts and design skills

You can nurture your child's understanding of the world with the following activities:

- Looking at and studying pictures
- Photography
- Making 3D projects
- Painting
- Drawing
- Using charts
- Mark making
- Sketching
- Pattern making
- Visual puzzles
- Humming, rhyming and singing
- Rapping
- Playing background music
- Patterns
- Form
- Playing instruments
- Tapping out poetic rhythms

Being creative can put you into a different mindset. You can get in a zone where you're fully focused, engrossed, and lose track of time. In a world that's becomingly increasing digital and tech developments increase the time we spend in front of a screen, there are fewer opportunities to play with the tangible.

Art and design is unique in its ability to allow you to take an idea, create it, and then hold the outcome in your hands in a relatively short space of time.

So don't underestimate the benefits of what seems like a simple process!

As we have shown, the advantages of bringing your ideas to life are huge! Best of all, done in a positive and nurturing way there's oodles of fun to be had as well!

Enjoy getting stuck into these activities.

Make a one-minute movie

Creating a story and exploring plots and characters can help your child to develop and organise their ideas coherently and creatively.

Nowadays, there are lots of devices that make it easy to record a short movie. A smartphone is a great tool to start with and as your child gets older, they can get behind the camera. Start the movie by inviting your child to think about the location for the film and who/what will feature. A storyboard is a great tool to capture ideas and ensure the script flows in a logical and interesting way. Once the story is planned your child can play it out using props etc. to bring their ideas to life.

Time needed 45min +

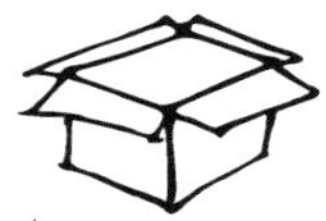

Items needed

A camera or smartphone, paper and pens, props and actors.

Adapt for younger children:
As children love seeing photos and videos of themselves, this activity helps build their self-confidence and self-esteem. You could help them make a recording of a story with their toys. They may also enjoy being in their own movie too.

Adapt for older children:
Your child will have fun doing this activity with their friends or siblings. Together they can develop and create a storyboard, before taking on different roles such as director, camera person and editor to bring the story to life. As a quick reminder, if you're uploading the film to the internet, check that the participants and their parents are happy for it to go online.

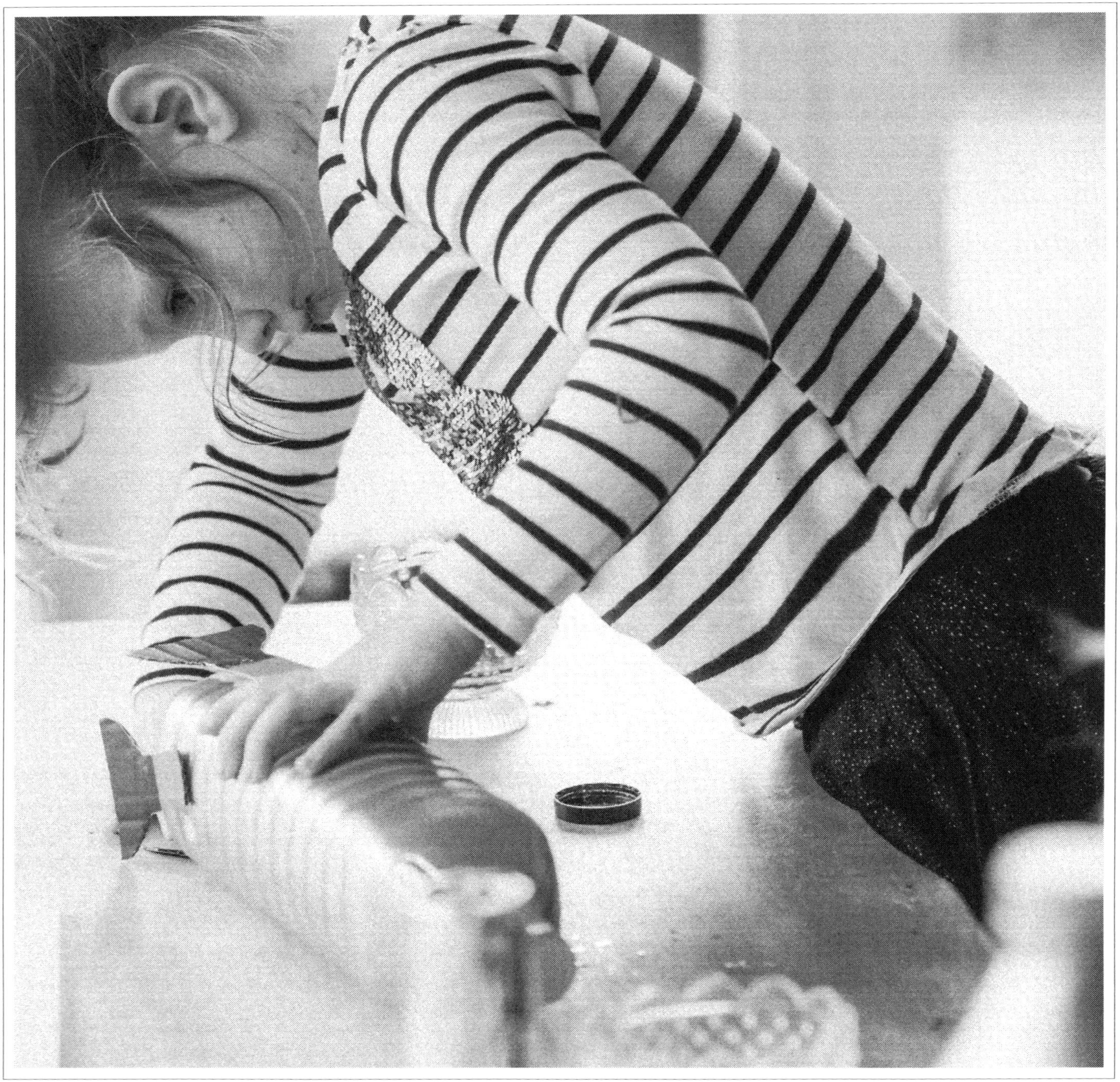

Create a 3D sculpture

Familiarisation with 3D shapes and structures helps your child to develop their spatial awareness and their understanding of how different shapes can be used to build a new construction.

When it comes to 3D sculptures, your child can explore all manner of materials from boxes and containers in the recycling bin, to blocks, straws and dried foods. Simply add glue or sticky tape and they can sculpture away. Remember natural building resources too. Depending on the time of year you could make a sand sculpture at the beach or a snow sculpture during the winter.

We have fond memories of Ollie's summer sand heroes. They were pyramid-like structures decorated with lots of shells and stones. He always made them when we were at the beach. Then in the winter, we made big snowmen and little snow heroes, creatures with twigs and stones for eyes. Natural materials also open up conversations about weather or tides. For example, you can talk about what happens to the snow when it melts or to the sand when the tide comes in.

Time needed

45min +

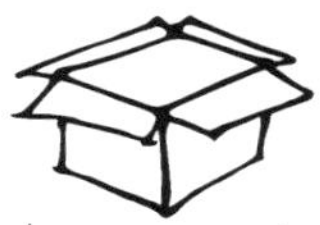

Items needed

Sand or snow, boxes, straws, blocks, brushes, paint, sequins and glue.

Adapt for younger children:
An alternative approach to this activity is to set your child on a treasure trail walk, which can be indoors or outdoors. Encourage them to collect their favourite objects and then watch them assemble the items into a 3D tower or sculpture.

Adapt for older children:
Older children can also collect favourite items, but give them longer to do so before making their sculpture. This helps children develop their patience and teaches them that not everything is instant and that it can be good to wait.

Idea 28

Take a line for a walk

This simple activity encourages concentration by allowing your child to experiment with the different shapes and patterns they can make with a single line.

This activity can be enjoyed by kids of all ages. Take a piece of paper and let your child choose from a range of pencils or pens. Starting at one place, invite your child to draw a line without taking their pen or pencil off the paper. You can set a time limit or just let your child continue the line for as long as they wish.

Once your child has finished, talk about what their line looks like. You can also encourage your child to colour in the spaces they've created with different colours or with patterns.

Time needed 15min +

Items needed: Paper or lining paper, pens, pencils, crayons, felt pens, gel pens and biros.

Adapt for younger children:
Use thick washable markers or paint dabbers to help them control their mark making. Once they get the idea then try different sized crayons and pens.

Adapt for older children:
Older children may enjoy creating more detailed images using a biro. This is also an activity they can do with their friends. Give each child a different colour and encourage them to overlap each other's lines to create a collective masterpiece.

Idea 29

Collect conkers and pine cones

This lovely activity inspires your child to explore in the fresh air. Not only will they learn more about the world, but they'll discover how to transform objects into something new.

Challenge your child to collect conkers and pine cones during a nature walk. As you walk, ask your child to think about why there are so many different seeds and leaves. In addition, discuss woodland safety too by talking about what items are good to touch and which should be avoided (for example, unless you're an expert on fungi, I'd recommend not touching mushrooms.)

Back home, use these natural art tools for rolling, painting, and printing to create some woodland art. In addition, you could transform the conkers and cones into little models. Simply get some pipe cleaners, wiggly eyes, feathers and anything else you've got to hand to see what creations your child and you can make together.

Time needed: 1hr +

Items needed: Conkers and pine cones, brushes, paints, glue, googly eyes and sequins.

Adapt for younger children:
Give your child a small cardboard box containing a piece of paper. Let them squirt some paint on top of the paper. Finally, give them a conker or a pine cone and let them move the box around. As the conker or cone rolls over the paint it will create some art on the underlying paper and be transformed itself.

Adapt for older children:
Encourage your child to create a woodland family by transforming the conkers or cones into little creatures. They can use a cardboard box too to create a backdrop for the friends.

idEA 30

Spot the difference

This simple game helps develop your child's memory. And if you reverse the roles, your child can test your recall skills too.

Ask your child to collect a number of objects and lay them out. Cover the collection with a blanket and ask your child which items they can remember. Next, try removing some of the pieces and see if they notice which ones have been taken away.

Adapt for younger children:
Reduce the number of items to three to start with so they get a sense of achievement and satisfaction. Ask them if they would like you to add another item or to find three other objects so the game can continue.

Adapt for older children:
Identify the ideal number of items for your child (that gives them a chance of succeeding) by trying different amounts.

Items needed

A tray, cloth to cover the tray, items to memorise.

Time needed

30min +

Enhanced recall skills

Encourage your child to associate the items with a journey or different parts of a room. For example, if there were four items (such as a watch, brush, teaspoon and a phone) you can picture these in your mind as larger or brighter or doing funny things.

Ask your child to imagine that they're entering their home.

- At the entrance you might have to brush past a huge brush because it's taking up the whole entrance
- As you walk into the hallway there's really loud tick tock noises and you see a tiny watch on the carpet
- In the kitchen you notice teaspoons on every countertop
- As you step into the garden the grass has been replaced by a huge phone screen

Once you've taken some time to create funny and memorable images with the objects and associated them with a physical journey, you'll find the objects are far easier to recall. Every person will have their own way of creating their own funny image journeys and it's a giggle to share these at the end.

I was fortunate to meet David Thomas – the world memory champion. I attended one of his workshops with Duncan and my boys. Within two days Ollie could remember a whole pack of shuffled cards! Here's another simple activity to try at home or with friends:

- Give everyone a pen and paper
- Read out 20 items (you'll want to write these down so you don't forget)
- Then ask everyone to recall and write down as many as they can
- Give people about 3-4 minutes to write down what they can remember
- Reread your list and ask everyone to score how many they got right

Then explain how to do the 'funny journey association'. Read out the list again and ask people to write down the items. See how many more items people remembered using this technique.

Be a master builder

Construction games help children develop a whole range of skills, from hand-eye coordination, to understanding how items fit together, to problem-solving skills. This activity also brings lots of self-satisfaction and pride as a child makes their vision a physical reality.

When it comes to building and construction, anything goes! Just use your imagination and remember to mix materials too.

Construction games are also brilliant for collaboration and can help forge strong family bonds. In our workshops, we often hear people sharing what creative building or modelling activities they have shared with their children. This activity also sparks stories about their own experiences playing as children. People said it was like a return to childhood.

Adapt for younger children:
Part of the building fun is knocking it all down. Have a go at using a range of building blocks to help your child see how many they can stack before the tower or construction falls over.

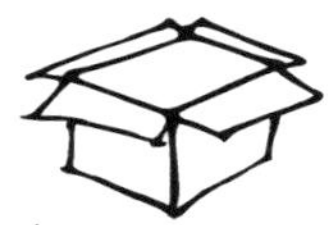

Items needed

Duplo, Lego, boxes from recycling, ice cubes, cushions, paper cups, lollipop sticks. You choose.

Adapt for older children:
A session we run with our after-school clubs is a building task using marshmallows and dried spaghetti. The children love creating shapes and sculptures with these unusual materials. And there's usually a few marshmallows left over for a treat at the end too.

Time needed

1hr +

We sometimes run themed weeks in partnerships with well-known brands. We've teamed up with great companies to provide our franchise owners with great resources and to provide our customers with great creative experiences. For instance, we ran a week of LEGO DUPLO sessions across the country with over 70,000 families.

We've also worked with the nice folks at Hasbro and developed lots of creative sessions using Play-Doh. Our sessions involved over 85,000 people involved in the activities and over 425,000 involved in social media.

Idea 32

Create a treasure map

This activity helps develop problem-solving skills as well as encouraging your child to follow instructions. It's fun too! Who doesn't enjoy a good adventure?

Turn your home or garden into the site of a big adventure by making your own treasure map. When drawing, ensure your map has all the significant objects or landmarks. If your treasure hunt is indoors you might include furniture and if the hunt is outside, include the trees or the shed etc. Finally, place a big X to show where the treasure is located. This helps children to orientate themselves and also to work out where they need to go next. Once drawn, make the map look ancient by ripping the edges, staining with cold, moist tea bags, and adding aged spots with coffee granules. Pop onto the radiator to dry.

Finally, make the treasure something your child will be excited to find. Something we enjoy is hiding chocolate eggs for our annual chocolate egg hunt. Alternatively, you could hide chocolate coins in a chest.

Adapt for younger children:
Create a treasure map that allows children to go on a shape hunt. As well as having fun, this activity builds your child's familiarisation with different shapes too.

Items needed

Paper, pens, crayons, cold tea bags, coffee granules and treasure to find.

Time needed

1hr +

Adapt for older children:
This activity works really well if you have a group of children. You can let them take turns figuring out the clues, or even have each child create the treasure trail and their own map. For a longer, more advanced trail leave a clue at the X spot to help your child find the next location:

'Where we keep all our muddy boots' – that could be the entrance to the house.

What gets wetter the more it dries?' – that could be a towel in the bathroom.

Idea 33

Music time

Music is integral to our lives. It can affect how we feel, entice us to move, and help us develop rhythm and coordination.

There are countless way to use music to inspire your children. For example, you can sing their favourite pop songs or nursery rhymes or you can have fun doing action songs. You can even encourage your child to make up their own songs complete with words and moves.

Music is woven into everything we do at The Creation Station. It's the reason we created an album designed to use music to nurture children's potential. I teamed up with the music editor of Hello magazine and talented singer songwriter, Jon Hogg to write and produce our music albums. We also teamed up with Mr Yipadee to provide fun and positive songs to use in our classes and for parents and carers to use at home.

The tracks cover a range of well-being and inspiring songs that are played in our sessions to get children to wiggle and jiggle along.

Time needed: 45min +

Items needed: Favourite music and voices.

Adapt for younger children:
Find out about music classes in your local community and join other adults and toddlers in musical fun. When it comes to singing and creating music with your own child, start with simple words that rhyme.

Adapt for older children:
There are lots of music classes for children that encourage your child to learn to play an instrument or two. When it comes to creating music from scratch, talk to your child about rhyme and rap. As you listen to a variety of songs encourage them to come up with their own versions.

Idea 34

Play rhythm games

Words, sounds and rhythm are all closely connected. Help your child explore these aspects of communication and develop their auditory and pattern skills.

Sit with your child and use prompts to explore different sounds and rhythms. Encourage your child to clap out syllables. You can even include some musical instruments such as shakers, triangles, tambourines, or drums.

Adapt for younger children:

- Pop some fruit and other small objects such as a car, plastic cup, and teddy bear into a bag
- Sit in a circle and ask your child to take out one object
- Then clap the name of the object based on the number of syllables. For example, ba-na-na would be three claps and car would be one clap

Items needed

Prompts to bring rhythm to life and musical instruments.

Time needed

30min +

Adapt for older children:

Words game like 'Keep the Beat' are great fun. This is how you play it:

- Sit in a circle and clap your hand two times and say, "Keep the beat"
- Then tap your knees twice
- Then clap your hands twice saying, "Girls' names" or "Boys' names"
- Then tap your knee twice
- Then the person on your right has to say a girl's name or boy's name with two beats in it (or if it was Barnaby it would have to be three claps.)
- Tap your knees twice then the next person has to say a child's name

And so it continues until someone claps out of time i.e. loses the beat or can't think of another name, fruit, country or whatever you like.

Five creative activities that encourage children to enjoy a variety of foods

You can nurture your child's physical development through the following activities:

- Take children supermarket shopping and talk about the foods they see
- Encourage them to help you prepare meals
- Bake together
- Explore ingredients
- Talk about taste and textures
- Picnics and nibble foods
- Allow children to play with food

At some point, every parent worries about what their child eats. 'Fussy eaters' are a common concern where a child is reluctant to try anything new. Some children seem to be averse to vegetables or anything green.

The key is to not worry too much. It's natural for children to reject new flavours and textures, so don't take it personally if your child spits your beautifully made spinach puree in disgust.

Research suggests that from the age of around 16 months babies can be more averse to trying new flavours so it's good to get them used to trying new things at an early age. It's interesting to note that your own facial expressions and body language have a significant effect on how your child copes with new experiences. It's worth thinking about your own reaction when supporting your child.

That said, childhood obesity is on the rise and research shows that if children are given a wide range of foods at an early age, it can help them eat a more varied diet. Do let your child explore a variety of textures and tastes from an early age. Here are some activities and ideas to help you do that.

Idea 35

Tricky taste game

Allowing children to differentiate between different flavours and to explain what they're tasting can help them understand more about their own preferences as well as inspiring them to try new foods in the future.

In a recent Channel 4 documentary called The Food Doctor, some of the children in The Creation Station Baby Discover classes got involved in an experiment. They were invited to taste foods with different textures and smells to see which affected them the most. The results indicated that involving your baby in a variety of textures at an early age can help them adapt to the range of different foods. We have seen this first hand with the both the babies and toddlers who come along to our classes. Supporting your child to explore different safe materials with their senses can help them overcome food dislikes and try new foods.

You can try something similar at home with the 'tricky taste' game. This helps children learn about different tastes and the role of our taste buds. Invite your child to taste each food item and then talk to them about what they think.

Time needed: 30min +

Items needed: Salt in water for a salty taste, sugar in water for a sugary taste, cold coffee for a bitter taste and lemons to taste for a sour taste.

Adapt for younger children:
Invite children to identify which other foods have a similar taste. Ask them to describe what they think of the flavours and identify which they like and dislike.

Adapt for older children:
You could invite your child to find out where the various flavours are tested on the tongue. They could even draw their own tongue map. You could also ask children to find other foods that have the same flavour. In addition, encourage your child to explore the range of different flavours through cooking and baking.

idEA 36

Print cards with vegetables

A lovely way to help your child feel familiar with and get used to different foods is to touch them and look at them closely. You can achieve this with vegetable prints.

Choose a selection of vegetables and turn them into stampers and paint rollers. A carrot with the end cut off makes an interesting paint roller and a stamper and a potato is big enough to carve out some interesting and unique shapes.

You can also use this activity to encourage colour awareness by allowing your children to mix their own colours. For example, take the primary colours of red, yellow, and blue. Then help your child to experiment by mixing different combinations to create the secondary colours of orange, purple, and green.

Adapt for younger children:
Extend a 'foodie' story. Here's how to make a caterpillar with savoy cabbage prints.

1. Take four circles of card, approximately 10 cm in diameter
2. Print with the bumpy side of the cabbage leaf onto the circle
3. Attach the circles with a stapler or with a split pin
4. Add two large eyes
5. Make two holes at the top of the head and cut a pipe cleaner in half
6. Thread the pipe cleaners through the holes to create your very own hungry caterpillar

Items needed

Selection of 'hard' vegetables such as potatoes, carrots, broccoli, cauliflower, paints and a knife. (Supervision needed).

Time needed

30min +

Adapt for older children:
Cut a potato in half and press a cookie cutter into the exposed white side. Use a knife to cut away the excess on the outside. With the cutter removed, you're left with a beautiful shape.

Make and play with gloop

If your little one feels comfortable exploring different textures, they're more likely to try foods that look, feel, and taste different. This activity can help your child feel more adventurous at mealtimes.

Gloop is super easy to make and feels interesting to play with. What's more, because it washes off easily you can get stuck in without worrying too much about the mess!

This is one of the strangest and most wonderful activities to do with children and as an adult you will probably find it fascinating. We know about solids and liquids, don't we? We know if you freeze water you get solid ice, right? Well gloop is a little different because this mixture transforms from a solid to liquid through the energy created by movement.

Here's how to make it:

1. Mix corn flour and water to get a thick paste
2. Then roll the paste in your hand to form a ball
3. Hold the ball in your hand and just wait to see what happens. I don't want to ruin the surprise!

Time needed

1hr 30min +

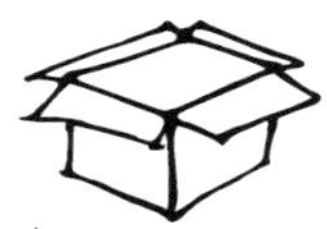

Items needed

Cornflour, water and paint.

Adapt for younger children:
An easy way to extend this activity is to colour the gloop with a squirt of paint. Then you can make some artwork by dripping the gloop onto paper. Black paper works really well for this because the colour contrasts really well. You can also experiment with different cutters and tools to see what happens.

Adapt for older children:
Ask them to think about why the gloop changes state as they play with it.

Gloop has thixotropic properties. This means the bonds are loose between the atoms, so they roll over each other easily to change their physical state.

Idea 38

Bake together

Baking gives your child the opportunity to practice and develop a whole range of skills. What's more, there's a tasty treat which everyone can enjoy at the end!

When you make food with your child, you engage in a whole host of activities together including selecting ingredients, weighing, mixing and pouring, time setting and waiting (and therefore patience), describing smells and textures, and of course, the pride and joy of eating what you've made!

Baking also helps children understand how items change through different effects – for example, through heat or when combined with other materials.

This activity can also encourage your children to try foods they wouldn't normally pick. As we know, children have a tendency to choose sweet foods, so bakes such as carrot cake are a great way to tempt your child to explore something different.

Time needed: 1hr +

Items needed: A recipe, ingredients, space in the kitchen.

Adapt for younger children:
Start with something simple such as decorating fairy cakes with icing sugar and water and sprinkles. Then progress to making chocolate krispies by mixing melted chocolate with rice cereal. Remember to discuss the different textures as you go along such as dripping, wet, dry, crunchy, sticky and mmm... licky! Ask your child to think of words that describe what they are doing too.

Adapt for older children:
Encourage your child to research and explore some recipes online or in books. Plan and organise the ingredients and tools. Measure the items and use a stopwatch to measure the time.

Idea 39

fruits and vegetable superheroes

Encouraging children to turns food into creatures and superheroes is not only fun, but an entertaining way to teach them about the nutritional value of different fruits and vegetables.

This activity is inspired by a chat show. I can still remember the train journey from Devon to London when I carried the strangest contents in my bag. I was preparing for my chat show appearance where I'd be talking about spooky vegetables! I had carrots, potatoes and parsnips with googly eyes, fangs and capes!

All you need is some fruit and vegetables, and with a bit of imagination you can transform them into your own superheroes with special powers inspired by the nutritional content of different foods. Carrots can have night vision and potatoes can be packed with energy. You can create a story or movie with characters. You can even help your child make their own superhero costume, so they can dress up too!

Time needed: 1hr +

Items needed: Fruit and vegetables, matchsticks, split pins or cocktail sticks.

Adapt for younger children:
Talk with your child about which character they liked best and which 'Super veggie' they'd like to make and why. You could also encourage your child to play a game where their superhero saves some of their other toys.

Adapt for older children:
Older children may be more interested in the nutritional angle that this activity opens up. Encourage them to spend longer with their food research so that they can create a collection of superheroes – all with different nutritionally based super powers. With their collection complete, older children may like to turn their characters into a story or a comic. Extend this activity by encouraging children to use other food items, such as grapes, beans etc.

Five creative activities that encourage you and your children to play together

You can nurture your child's physical development through the following activities:

- Rounders or football
- Card games
- Family meetings
- Obstacle courses
- Large group mural on lining paper cook, eat and clear up together
- Build a marshmallow and dry spaghetti tower
- Go on a treasure hunt
- Parachute games
- Singing and action songs
- Plan a meal, shop for the items

Life requires you to get on with people. So, helping your child to respect others' opinions and ideas is a good skill to develop. It's not about getting your own way all the time, but about taking turns and recognising that other people's opinions are valued and important too.

One of the best things about creative arts and crafts is you can adapt activities for all ages.

Whether you're nine months, nine years, or ninety years, you can have fun exploring your ideas and creating something new. That's why creative fun is a great activity to enjoy as a group.

Whether that's with friends, siblings, or a whole family, doing creative things together provides fun and fosters a sense of group achievement.

We often run school collaborative projects when we provide art days. It's great to see all the kids working together. We now do this with groups within care homes and the sense of fulfilment from everyone involved is fantastic.

The activities in this section can be explored at home. Everyone can join in so it's a great inclusive activity. If you're looking for ways to increase family bonds, reduce sibling tension, and create harmony – while developing everyone's creative side – the following activities can help.

Create your family guide

Creating the positive framework that you want to have for your home is a hugely valuable activity that you can do together.

As parents, we often find ourselves saying, "Don't do that". There's usually a good intention. We want to keep our children safe, prevent them from making a mistake, or avoid a pile of mess! But the payoff is we often focus on the negative. We say the thing we don't want our children to do rather than articulating and reinforcing the positive behaviour that we DO want them to adopt. For example, instead of saying, "Don't run across the road" you could flip it and say, "Stay near me please."

When we choose to talk from the positive angle, it allows children to focus (and practise) the behaviours we do want them to have. A really good way of putting this principle into practice is with your family guide. Work together to create a set of values and behaviours you'd like to have in your home and then pin it up where everyone can see it daily. For example, ours is displayed on the boiler door and because we all see the guide every day, it's a powerful reminder of how everyone is expected to behave and interact together.

What positive framework do you have in your home? Why not create your own family guide together? It could change the atmosphere of your home and help to build respect amongst family members.

Adapt for younger children:
Invite children to express your family's values through their own pictures, which you can include on your family guide. Bring your guide into the conversation frequently to help reinforce the behaviours you want to see as your child's awareness and understanding grows.

Adapt for older children:
As an extension, encourage a values guide to outline what it is they expect of themselves. This can be a powerful way to develop responsibility and self-awareness.

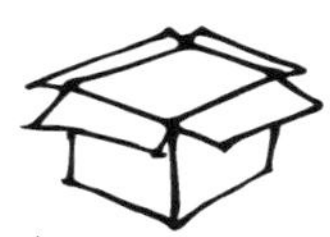

Items needed

A family meeting to discuss and agree what should be on your guide. Paper, felt pens, glue, sequins and your favourite embellishments.

Time needed

1hr +

Idea 41

Play word association games

Games offer a great opportunity to help children develop their social skills and learn about taking turns and winning and losing. And they're lots of fun too!

These simple word association games can also help little ones develop their language and communication skills.

Adapt for younger children:
Try playing 'Granny went to market'. Start the game with the phrase, "Granny went to the market and bought a..."

Each player takes a turn to add a new item to granny's shopping basket, while recapping the other things she's already bought. This game is great for encouraging recall and memory.

Items needed

Pens, pencils and paper.
Friends or family to play with.

Time needed

30min +

Adapt for older children:
Play word consequences. Here's how:

- Everyone has a piece of paper and writes the first line – a boy's name
- Then the paper is folded over and passed to the next person – they have to write a girl's name
- The paper is folded over again and the next part of the story is written – what clothes he was wearing
- Fold again, pass around and write down what she was wearing
- Another fold and write where they met
- A final fold and write what happened next
- Then unfold the page and read the crazy story aloud

A fun alternative to the word consequence game is pass the picture. The process is the same as above, but instead of using words you use a picture, so the first section is a hat, then the face, the torso, the legs, and finally the feet. Younger children can play this too.

Idea 42

Create a family quiz

A big quiz is a great way to connect all ages together in a fun activity. At our recent 20th wedding anniversary/birthday party bash, my eldest Sam and my sister Fran created a family quiz, which was hilarious.

Decide the format of your quiz. If you're quizzing with different age groups, remember to make your questions inclusive so everyone can take part. It's fun coming up with your own questions, but you can always download quizzes online if you get stuck.

You could expand this activity by creating prizes (or forfeits!) and you can also create different roles such as team captains, quiz master, timekeeper, and scorer etc. You could also create team badges or banners and even create home-made buzzers. Anything goes so just have fun.

Time needed 45min +

Items needed Quiz format/rules, questions and answers, pens and paper.

Adapt for younger children:
Create simple questions which your younger child can answer such as:

- Who's wearing a red T-shirt?
- Who's got the longest hair?
- What fruit is yellow etc.?

Once you've played the game and your child understands how it works you can ask if they'd like to have a go at being the quiz master.

Adapt for older children:
Encourage your child to create the quiz, take the role as quiz master, ask the questions, and keep score.

Idea 43

Stone art

This is another fun activity that inspires children to transform an everyday object that they find when they're exploring outside.

Take a bag to the beach, or the park. Collect stones to take home and create stone art together. Take your time to find the perfect stone. Maybe pick an interesting or an unusual shape or a stone that's especially large. See what ideas spark your imagination while you're combing across the shores for the perfect blank canvas.

It's worth checking you're allowed to take stones home. In some places you are asked to leave the beach intact.

Adapt for younger children:
Try painting the stone to create a rock pet.

Items needed

Stones, paints, sequins, googly eyes and felt pens.

Time needed

30min +

Adapt for older children:
Use the stone as a canvas to paint on. You could also try stacking the rocks to create a tower. You may want to experiment with Blu Tack to see if you can attach the rocks together in a way that challenges gravity!

Try cutting brightly coloured letters from magazines and gluing them onto a washed and dry smooth stone.

You could also create the letters from scratch by drawing them. Remember to paint over the stone with PVA glue when it's dry to seal the stone.

Idea 44

Collaborate

One of the best things about creative activities is EVERYONE can join in – regardless of age and ability. When it comes to your imagination, anything goes which means arts and crafts is a simple yet effective way to do something as a family.

Decide upon a group task and then work together to create a masterpiece that everyone has contributed towards. Here are some ideas:

1. Grab a long piece of lining paper and give everyone some pens to brainstorm ideas
2. Gather rocks and sticks and make a collaborative sculpture on your walk or at home
3. Make a model together and ensure everyone joins in
4. Create a meal where someone makes the starter, someone the main, and someone else the pudding – and wash up after
5. Give everyone three resources and see what they can create. When you limit the range of materials, it encourages your child to focus and think differently. In the example below, we gave children egg boxes, wiggly eyes, and paint.
6. Collect some toys and other household items, dip them into paint and make a big piece of collaborative artwork on some lining paper

Adapt for younger children:
Use this idea as a way to show children that they can play a role in everything. This is a great way to build their self-esteem and encourage teamwork.

Adapt for older children:
Give older children more responsibility. For example, they can be encouraged to take on some leadership tasks, such as helping a younger sibling, they could be in charge of leading a discussion to choose which activity you'll collaborate on.

Time needed: 1hr+

Items needed: Select what you need depending on the activities chosen.

rather be a ....

Idea 45

Plant flowers in a pot

As well as introducing your child to a range of plants and exploring how they grow, this activity allows you to get really creative over your choice of plant pot too.

First do some research to determine what plants or vegetables you'd like to grow. Your choice will depend on things such as space and whether you'll be growing your plants indoors or outside.

With plants chosen, pick some pots and containers. This is where you can get creative. For example, you could choose pots based on what the plants look like. Alternatively, use this activity as an opportunity to recycle and transform objects that have previously been used for something else.

Time needed 45min +

Items needed
Seeds or plants, pots, containers, compost and a watering can.

Adapt for younger children:
Have a go at planting sunflower seeds and measuring how they grow or plant some cress and make a cress head.

Adapt for older children:
There are lots of different plant pot containers you can use. Try brainstorming different ideas to discover alternative containers.

A mystery tour picnic

Combine a day of adventure with a fun picnic to create plenty of memories and lots of talking points. When you're out and about remember to weave in some of the other outdoor activities contained in this book.

One of my favourite memories from growing up was when mum took us out on a mystery tour. It was so exciting because we never knew where we'd end up! We'd have our hard-boiled eggs and sandwiches ready and find somewhere interesting and new to enjoy our picnic. One day we even had our picnic in a lay-by on the side of a road and then just came back! Sometimes the location didn't matter, it was just great to all be together.

It wasn't until I was a bit older that I realised they were called mystery tours just in case we didn't end up where we were supposed to be going! It was always an adventure and the picnic was the icing on the cake.

Time needed 1hr +

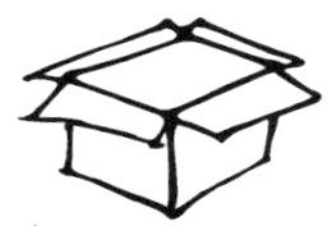

Items needed

A yummy picnic. An idea of where you'd like to eat it! The means to get you there – whether that's walking, cycling, driving, or going by train.

Adapt for younger children:
Hard boil some eggs. When cooled draw funny faces on the eggs in felt pen. Let your child smash the eggs and mash them with some mayonnaise. Prepare some sandwiches and fruit together and pop in a bag to take for your picnic.

Adapt for older children:
Encourage your child to think about your picnic menu and get them involved in shopping and preparing the picnic.

Idea 47

Make a kite

You can make a kite on a rainy day and then take it with you when the rain has stopped, and the wind is blowing. This fun activity is also a good conversation starter to pique children's curiosity about the weather.

There are lots of different ways you can make a colourful kite.

Here's a great method that uses sticky-back plastic:

1. Cut out two diamond shapes about 35cm long
2. Add some coloured paper and put strips of black paper around the edge
3. Add pipe cleaners or more black paper to make the cross in the middle
4. Use a long piece of ribbon or lots of pipe cleaners for the tail
5. Pop the other diamond shaped sticky-back plastic on top of the piece with the collage materials and stick the two pieces together

You can add cut up straws, buttons or cellophane to create a fancy tail.

Time needed: 45min +

Items needed: Sticky-back plastic, coloured paper, pipe cleaners, ribbon, straws, buttons and cellophane for the tail.

Adapt for younger children:
Take your kite out for an adventure and test the kite under different weather conditions.
Ask your child to identify when the kite will or won't fly.

Adapt for older children:
Encourage your child to experiment with different shapes and sizes of kite and also different tails so they can figure out what flies best.

Five easy, low-cost activity ideas to inspire your child on a rainy day

You can nurture your child's physical development through the following activities:

- Play board games
- Indoor hide-and-seek
- Have hand and feet massage sessions
- Create food container boats for puddles
- Make greeting cards
- Pop waterproofs on and go for a splash

Enjoying creative fun doesn't have to be expensive because you can use the resources you have to hand.

There are a few handy essentials worth having in stock. These include:

Brushes, water-based glue, masking tape, overalls, paint (ready mixed or washable paint), crayons, coloured pencils, scissors, googly eyes, double-sided tape, a single hole punch, stapler, and a pencil sharpener.

We have put together a little 'Essential toolkit' with storage boxes on The Creation Station website which is very popular.

Armed with your toolkit and your child's imagination, there's plenty you can do to make a rainy day stress-free and full of fun – without breaking the bank.

Make your own newspaper creations

Want something to do with that pile of old newspapers? Add in some imagination and you'll be surprised what you can transform a few balls of scrunched up paper into.

An easy way to create a creature is to scrunch up some newspaper into a ball and then cover with masking tape. You can add a head, arms, and legs if you want. Finally, join all the pieces together with masking tape and paint in any colour or pattern your child wants. When your child's creation is dry, you can cover it with PVA glue to make the creature waterproof and shiny. And for a super shiny effect, paint with wood varnish.

Time needed 1hr +

Items needed: Newspaper, masking tape, paint PVA glue and wood varnish (Optional).

Adapt for younger children:
Create a collection of newspaper creatures and use them as characters in a made-up story or a start-from-scratch song. Encourage your child to give their creature a name and to tell you about its life.

Adapt for older children:
Older children can be encouraged to take more time over their creation and even make something more ambitious.

Another alternative is to use the newspaper with wallpaper paste and make your own papier mâché. The cheeky cat on the right was popular when I used to sell my papier mâché sculptures in the past.

Some of my fun artworks over the years

Create with nature

The great outdoors is teeming with ideas to spark your child's imagination. From materials to create with, to views that inspire a masterpiece, interacting with the natural world can develop your child's creativity immensely. The artist Andy Goldsworthy creates stunning outdoor sculptures so you could research what type of activities he does and gain inspiration from his work.

There are countless things you can create with natural materials. What's more, you can adapt to suit the needs, interests, and talents of your child.

Clay leaf prints
Place the leaf onto some clay and then 'age' the clay with coffee granules. You can try pressing the different sides of the leaf to create different effects.

3D sculptures
Using twigs you've collected tie them together to create a tepee and create your own mini nature den. Think about who could live there and what would they need. Will it be a home for animals or mini humans?

Nature Raft
Create your own nature survival raft. Think about the items you could use for the sail and what you might need on your raft.

Twig art
Collect leaves and twigs and other woodland treasures to create a portrait. You can extend this activity by creating a life story for your character.

Nature mobile
Gather a selection of your favourite nature found items and tie them onto string to create a mobile.

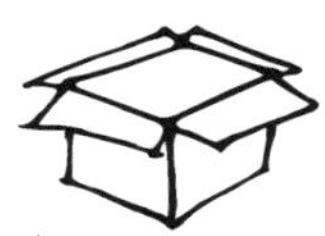

Items needed

Items found in the garden.

Time needed

30min +

Idea 50

Make a paper plane

Folding paper aeroplanes helps children develop their dexterity. When this activity is done with other children it also injects some healthy competition too. Problem-solving skills as well as cause and effect are also stimulated as children experiment and explore to figure out which design works best.

Using different colours and textures of paper, fold a paper aeroplane and see how far you can make it fly. Next, create some other flying origami projects to explore aerodynamics.

Time needed 15min +

Items needed

Different types of paper to fold with pencils and pens to decorate.

Adapt for younger children:
Show your children how to fold the paper and create a crease by rubbing your hands over the edge of the fold. Show them how this helps to hold the fold in place. The amount of pressure you apply affects the fold.

Adapt for older children:
Encourage your children to experiment with different designs and folds. You could have a competition to see which design works the best and what adaptations help or hinder the flight.

You can also play target practice with paper. Choose some cups and screw up some paper, or foil, to make a ball. Line up the cups and FIRE!

Idea 51

Make a see-through, crunchy bag

There are a wealth of activities to be enjoyed using everyday household materials. At The Creation Station we often turn the ordinary into the extraordinary, just by thinking about it slightly differently.

Here's an activity that is really simple, yet really allows for imaginations to come to life.

- Take a piece of cling film and place a layer of wrappers and paper on top
- Place another piece of cling film of the same size on top
- Add a layer of different items such as feathers or sequins
- Place a piece of cling film on top
- Fold the edge over and use sticky tape
- Pop a thin strip of cardboard across the top to make a handle

Time needed: 30min +

Items needed: Cling film, a selection of wrappers and paper, sticky tape, feathers, glitter, sequins, buttons, beads and cardboard.

Adapt for younger children:
You could use a zip lock bag and encourage them to find things that are crunchy that can go in their crunchy bag.

Adapt for older children:
Ask your child how they would adapt this to create a different type of bag such as a shiny bag or a red bag. Encourage and celebrate their ideas.

Idea 52

Salty paint

This activity has its roots in science and is a wonderful way to introduce your child to the magic of experimentation and discovery.

Dissolve lots of salt into warm water and stir until it disappears. Explore how much salt you can add before it stops dissolving. Then, with a paint brush, brush the salted water paint onto card and wait for it to dry. This works really well on black card because as the water evaporates and the card dries, you're left with a silvery glimmer on the page.

Time needed 45min +

Items needed: Salt, water, black card and paint brushes.

Adapt for younger children:
Talk about how this 'paint' looks like normal water, but that something magical will happen. Emphasise that the change won't happen automatically, but that it will take time. This helps your child develop patience and also to appreciate that many things don't happen immediately.

Remember to check the paper every few hours so your child can see the transformation for themselves.

Adapt for older children:
Experiment with different sized paint brushes and draw a variety of different pictures with the salty paint. Older children will also be interested to understand how the transformation happened, so use this as an opportunity to talk about processes such as dissolving and evaporation.

Start creating and filling your blank canvas

> "It always seems impossible until it's done."
>
> ***Nelson Mandela***

When you nurture your own and your child's creativity, you'll unlock a magical world that allows your child to explore their creative sparks and express the wonder within.

I hope this book has inspired you and filled you with creative ideas to enrich the lives of you and your children. With the 52 activities included in this book you have plenty of ideas to explore. Of course this is just scratching the surface of the thousands of things you can do with your children to keep them inspired and to develop their all-important creative intelligence.

So here are some further resources for you to discover...

Grab our fortnightly creative tips

If you're keen to continue your creative journey, we'd love to help. The easiest way to do this is to visit our website and request to receive ideas, inspiration and special offers. In return, you'll receive our fortnightly creative emails which are packed with free tops tips and activities to keep your imagination stimulated.

You can receive your free tips at **www.creationstation.co.uk**

In addition, you'll find plenty of resources to stock up your arts and craft supplies in our online shop. And if you'd like to treat your kids to a monthly creative gift, check out our FAB Fun Arty Boxes, which brings The Creation Station ideas and resources direct to your front door.

Get involved

Whilst there's oodles of creative ideas you can explore at home, you may like to join one of our weekly classes and get creative with like-minded parents while your child mixes with children of a similar age. Or you may enjoy immersing yourself in some fun creative workshops yourself.

Over 1,000 classes, parties and events run across the UK every week - for all ages. There are new-born Tiny Treasures, Baby Discover, and Little Explorer preschool classes, as well as Create Clubs and school workshops, Arty Party birthdays, adult creative crafters, and now our Care and Creativity workshops for older people and our fabulous intergenerational workshops. In short, something for every age!

To find out what's happening in your area visit and pop in your postcode **www.thecreationstation.co.uk**

Creativity can and will change the world.

Ideas truly are the currency of the 21st century and although none of us can predict the future, we do know that things will change. Whether it's environmental, political, economic or social change, there has never been a more important time to equip our children and ourselves with the ability to explore, discover, and develop.

It's why I'm passionate about getting children excited about exploring their potential and I believe developing creative intelligence is a powerful way to unlock the wonder within.

A creative approach can spark the fire within and begin a journey that helps each child and adult shine brightly and truly glow.

Here's to inspiring futures.

Sarah

Acknowledgements

Writing a book, like so many things in life, involves the kind support and help of many many people.

Thanks to Georgina El Morshdy, Simon Ramsey, Julia Bodie, John Slater, Matt Austin, Terry Mohan and Richard May for helping me to get my ideas into the words, photos, and design of this book.

Thanks to all the fantastic children, parents, and careers who helped bring the 52 activities to life. Bea with Fleur and Fergus – you guys were brilliant! Kirsty Langdon Justice and Shelly Stammers – I know why the children love being with you. And a BIG special thank you to Ellie, Grace, Alfie, Sydney, Nelly Mathew and Beau.

Thanks to all the children and families that have attended Creation Station classes, parties, and events over the past sixteen years. I hope you've enjoyed a few creative sparks to share, treasure and grow from.

Thanks to all the venues, organisations, partners, charities, companies, agencies, brands and all our suppliers, trainers and coaches that we have had the privilege to work with. Special thanks go to the teams at the British Franchise Association and the Children's Activity Association. Thank you it's been fun!

Thanks to the many many friends and colleagues I've made and met along the way. I'd like to share big love and thanks to Jan Burrell, Elaine Mannix, Penny Pullan, Kerry and Dave Davison, Simon Hammett, Nicky and Barnaby Cat-Marrision, Caroline Catermull, Suzanne Dibble, Luc Floreani, John Wilkinson, John Hogg, Deano – Mr Yipadee, Nigel Botterill, Steven Frost, Sharon Weston, Ian Sharland, Amanda Gummer, Sam Willoughby, David Thomas, Gilly Sowden and Nik Heap, Julia Bramble, Celia Delaney, Tara Howard, Anne Walker, Chris Lorimer, Andy McCreadie, Chris Strong, Ruskin Wilson, Viv Pearce, Sally Johnson, Katharine Bourke, Phil Johnston, Sarah Knight, Shaun Durham, Pip Wilkins and Helen Thompson.

None of this would be possible without our incredible family of Creation Station Franchise Owners (in the order in which they joined us and accurate as of November 2017).

Jackie Farrow, Lisa Hagg, Nicki Smith, Penny Gilbert, Sue Hammond, Melanie Dawson, Naomi Savory, Catherine Stanley, Kevin Kerridge, Kirsty Hickson, Tracey Pennell, Nicole Norman, Clare Docherty, Julia Scoble, Emma Theunissen, Vikki Newman, Deepa Patel Robinson, Mita Pabari, Emma White, Claire Darnley, Kathryn Pownall, Louise Richardson, Sarah Ekins, Anna Quinn, Claire Lyon, Kirsty Cooper, Jenny Farmer, Suzie Smith, Abbie Melia, Melissa Millington, Melanie Jeffries, Sarah Cattley, Lisa Tye, Jann Thorpe, Nicola Cliffe, Paula Martin-King, Rebecca Dickinson, Rebecca Wootton, Emma Winterbourne, Debbie Kersley, Sonja Badenhorst, Hayley Cronin and Alex Parker, Stephanie Swan, Kirstie Ireland, Emma Hinkins,

Abi Cutler, Sarah Jones, Katy Williams, Fran Wilson, Kay Fletcher, Urmi Acharya, Louisa Theyers, Cheryl O'Connor, Sarah Burnett, Laurie Keating, Helen Naraine, Judith Coles, Catherine Scott, Farah Wahed, Victoria Rundle, Christina Turnbull, Joanna Cameron, Sharon Keirle, Sarah Codling, Emma Carter, Kirsty Tatum, Pornthida Crookes, Georgie Moore, Debs Richmond, Kirsty Ansell, Sharon Fisher, Alison Denning, Vicky Breakspear, Sandra Steele, Emma Dove, Kat Gillespie, Sam Walker, Tracey Ilett, Louisa Tasker, Sarah Jenkinson, Joscelin Hennigan, Helen Earnshaw, Karen Joyce, Yat-Chen Lee and Yat-On Lo, Carol Roylance, Fariyal Shariff, Hannah Martindale, Jo Le-Good, Heather Berry, Carolyn Anderson, Jo Jacobs, Emma Brooks, Rosie Oates, Beatrice Locock, Khadija Pieterson, Liz Pinder, Lisa Bosher, Rebecca McCarthy, Gurjot Kondral, Joanne Everby, Janna Tratt, Lorna Gittoes, Lucy Harris, Vibha Vagadia, Mishalle Deepchand, Hanli Bouwer, Ally Farrell, Kat Howard, Gill Rohan, Sarah Griffiths, Carys Harvey, Charlotte Eames, Sam Smith, Chantal Craig, Jayne Stafford, Brad Thompson, Jen Elfverson, Tracey Webb, Jo Reynolds, Claire Spencer, Tracy Prescott, Abby Newell, Deepti Mistry, Liza Cray, Mark Hugh-Jones, Reshma Menon-Jones, Sarah Firth, Vicky Whitwell, Ellie Hall and Vanessa Whitehouse.

And a special mention to Louise Radford, Anna Rossi and Ali Webb who were our very first franchise owners.

My thanks to our incredible franchise owners who also work as Business Development Managers and work on our Franchise Advisory Council Nicki Smith, Emma Theunissen, Jann Thorpe, Penny Gilbert, Louise Richardson, Bex Dickinson, Sharon Keirle, Jo Cameron, Julia Scoble, Kirsty Hickson, Nicole Norman, Ally Farrell and Debs Richmond.

And thanks to the awesome team at Creative Hub including Elaine Bowler, Richard Murrell, Alan Schaufler, Maggie Seager, Tash Budza, Sophie Seager, Sara le Roux, and Julie Brown. Thank you team – you all rock!

A massive thanks to my sis Fran Long who still fixes everything, manages our website (which we just won a national award for), and helps franchise owners and the Creative Hub team get through those tricky techy problems that we all encounter. Also to my siblings and partners, Hugh and Sue, George and Janice, Emily, and Paul and also Tracey.

My immeasurable thanks go to my mum and dad, Ann and George Long. Their belief and unconditional love for me has set me up to live a life where I continue to strive to do my best, make a difference, and live a fulfilled and happy life.

Duncan Cressall – my lovely hubby. Thank you for your continuing support, your patience with my mad schemes and ideas, guidance on strategy, and keeping true to our values. Couldn't have done this without you x

Finally to Sam, Ollie, and Josh – my incredible boys. Thank you for giving me the best job in the world, for teaching me things I never knew or thought I'd ever need to know, and for inspiring me to see the world with new eyes.

I'm so grateful for all the love, encouragement, faith and enthusiasm I've had from so many people.

Thanks to this long list of supporters, cheerleaders, and partners in creativity, we've been able to create, connect and inspire and do our bit to help children unlock the creative sparks they need to flourish and express the wonder within.

References

1. Dr Suess, (1990). Oh, The Places You'll Go! Random House

2. Frost, R. (1916). The Road Not Taken. Accessed 3rd Oct 2017 through https://www.poetryfoundation.org/poems/44272/the-road-not-taken

3. Coelho, P. (1995). The Alchemist. Harper Collins.

4. Gladwell, M. (2009). What the Dog Saw. Little, Brown and Company.

5. Wimmer & Perner. (1983). When Children Begin To Simulate Other Minds. Accessed August 2017 through http://www.spring.org.uk/2008/06/when-children-begin-to-simulate-other.php

6. Brodsky, S. (2017). The average mom reportedly works the equivalent of 2 full-time jobs per week. Accessed June 2017 through www.goodhousekeeping.com/life/parenting/news/a45318/average-mom-clocks-two-full-time-jobs/

7. Kipling, R. (1910). If. Accessed 2nd Nov 2017 through http://www.kiplingsociety.co.uk/poems_if.htm

8. Rodgers, L. The New Family Values. Accessed June 2017 through http://www.parenting.com/article/family-values

9. Atkins, S. (2013). The Sue Atkins Inspiring Sunday Saying. Accessed March 2017 through https://www.sueatkinsparentingcoach.com/2013/09/the-sue-atkins-inspiring-sunday-saying-53/

10. Duckworth, A. (2016). Grit: The Power of Passion and Perseverance. Vermilion.

11. Picasso, P. (1881-1973). Metamorphoses of the Human Form. Prestel-Verlag.

12. Møller, . (2005). Title. Accessed May 2017 through http://www.openwindows.se/ow2/doc/Claus_M/Creative_Intelligence-CMC[1].pdf

13. Gardner, H. (1993). Multiple Intelligences. Basic Books.

14. De Bono, E. (2016) Lateral Thinking: A Textbook of Creativity. Penguin Life.

15. Edwards, C, Gandini, L, Forman, G. (1998). Hundred Languages of Children: The Reggio Emilia Approach to Early Childhood Education. (2nd edition). Elsevier Science.

16. Robinson, K. (2010). The Element: How Finding Your Passion Changes Everything. Penguin.

17. Russ, S. (1996). Development of Creative Processes in Children. Wiley Online Library.

18. Wolf, G. (1996). Steve Jobs: The Next Insanely Great Thing. Accessed Aug 2017 through https://www.wired.com/1996/02/jobs-2/

19. Sharp, C. (2004). Developing young children's creativity: What can we learn from research. Accessed June 2017 through www.nfer.ac.uk/publications/55502/55502.pdf

20. Angelou, M. (1982). Interview for Bell Telephone Magazine. Accessed March 2017 through http://www.quotabelle.com/quote/you-cant-use-up-creativity-the

21. A, Roddick. (2002). Trade Justice: Anita Roddick. Accessed Aug 2017 through http://news.bbc.co.uk/1/hi/talking_point/forum/2050293.stm

22. Nussbaum, B. (2005). Get Creative! How to build creative companies. Accessed July 2017 through https://www.bloomberg.com/news/articles/2005-07-31/get-creative

23. The British Association for Early Years Education. (2012). Development Matters in the Early Years Foundation Stage. Accessed March 2016 through https://www.foundationyears.org.uk/files/2012/03/Development-Matters-FINAL-PRINT-AMENDED.pdf

24. Fulwiler, M. The Research: The Still Face Experiment. Accessed Aug 2017 through https://www.gottman.com/blog/the-research-the-still-face-experiment/

25. RSPB (s.d). Make a speedy bird cake. Accessed 2nd Nov 2017 through https://ww2.rspb.org.uk/fun-and-learning/for-kids/games-and-activities/activities/make-a-speedy-bird-cake

Bibliography/Further Reading

I'm very grateful to the following authors for the inspiration, knowledge and insight they've shared with me through their books and writings.

Branson, R. (2011). Screw It Let's Do It. Virgin Books.

Bruce, T. (2004). Cultivating Creativity. Hodder and Stoughton.

Churchill Dower, R. (Date). Nurturing Young Children's Learning through The Arts. Early Arts.

Covey, Stephen, R. (2004) Seven Habits of Highly Effective People. Simon and Schuster.

Craft, A. (2004). Creativity and Early Years Education. Continuum Books.

Dr Seuss (1990). Oh The Places You'll Go. Random House.

Essame, C. (2016). Fighting the dragon, finding the self. An introduction to why art and play matter in early childhood. Create-CATT

Everarda, E. A. (1999). Meta-analysis of research on creativity: the effects of instructional variables. Unpublished dissertation, Fordham University.

Earlyarts (2015). Nurturing Young Children's Learning through The Arts. Accessed 6th August 2017 through https://earlyarts.co.uk/teaching-packs.

Gerber, M. (2001). The E-myth Revisited. Harper Business.

Harris, Paul L. (2000). The Work of the Imagination. Wiley-Blackwell.

Gardner, H. (2011). Frames of Mind: The Theory of Multiple Intelligences. Basic Books.

Keller, G and Papasan, J. (2013). The One Thing. Bard Press.

Meador, K. (1992). Emerging Rainbows: A Review of the Literature on Creativity in Preschoolers. Sage Journals. (Vol 15, Issue 2, 1992).

Murdock, M. (2002). The effects of teaching programmes intended to stimulate creativity: a disciplinary view. Scandinavian Journal of Educational Research

Nussbaum, B. (2013). Creative Intelligence: Harnessing the Power to Create, Connect, and Inspire. HarperBusiness.

A, Roddick. (2005). Business As Unusual: My Entrepreneurial Journey, Profits with Principles. Anita Roddick Books

Runco, M. (1996). Creativity from Childhood through Adulthood: The Developmental Issues. New Directions for Child Development. Wiley Online Library

Tims, C. (Ed.) (2010) Born Creative London. DEMOS.

31985728R00186

Printed in Great Britain
by Amazon